Origami in Action

Paper Toys that Fly, Flap, Gobble, and Inflate!

by Robert J. Lang

Photography by Scott Griggs

St. Martin's Griffin
New York

For Peter

Also by Robert J. Lang

The Complete Book of Origami
Origami Zoo (with Stephen Weiss)
Origami Animals
Origami Sea Life (with John Montroll)
Origami Insects and Their Kin

ORIGAMI IN ACTION:
PAPER TOYS THAT FLY, FLAP, GOBBLE, AND INFLATE!
Copyright ©1997 by Robert J. Lang
Printed in the United States of America.
For information, address
St. Martin's Press
175 Fifth Avenue
New York, N.Y. 10010

Design by Robert J. Lang
Cover photos by Scott Griggs
Cover design by David Rotstein

Library of Congress Cataloging-in-Publication Data

Lang, Robert J.
    Origami in action : paper toys that fly, flap, gobble, and inflate! /
Robert J. Lang. — First St. Martin's Griffin ed.
    p. cm.
    ISBN 0-312-15618-9
    1. Origami 2. Paper toy making. I. Title.
TT870.L2615 1997
736'.982—dc21   96-53504
                                                                CIP

First St. Martin's Griffin Edition: June 1997

10 9 8 7 6 5 4

Table of Contents

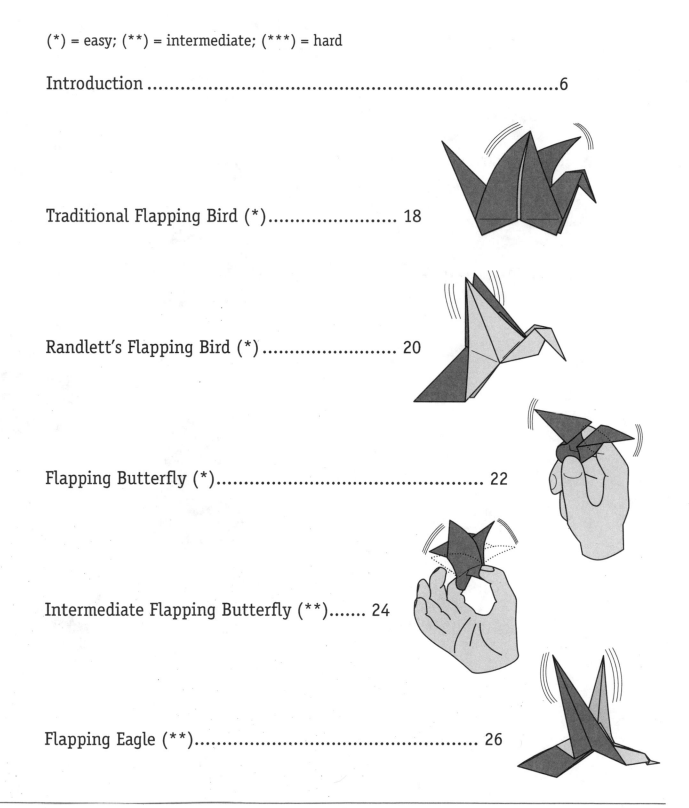

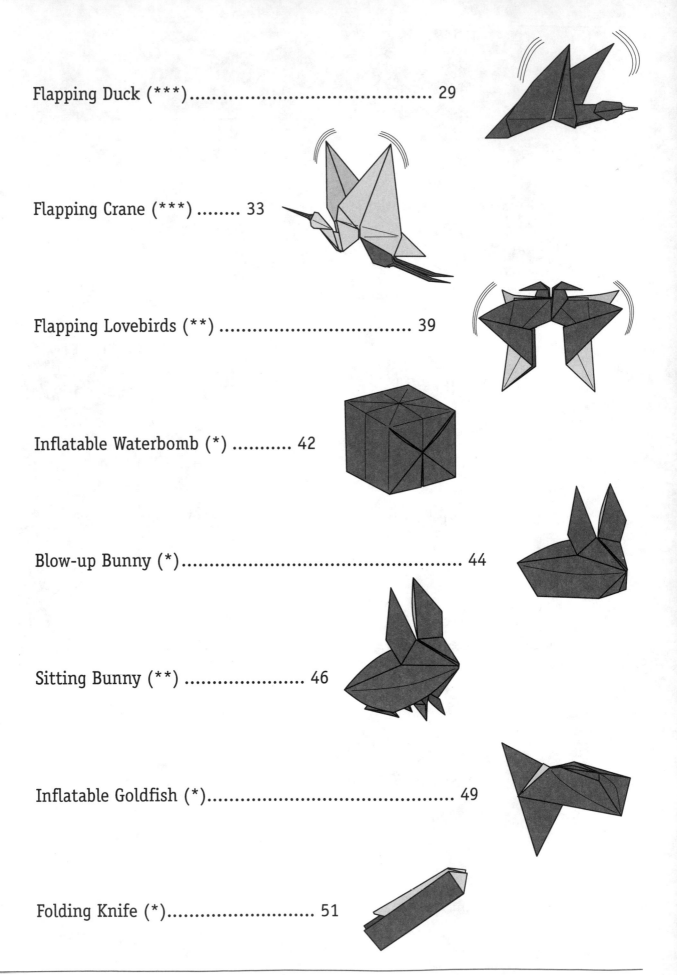

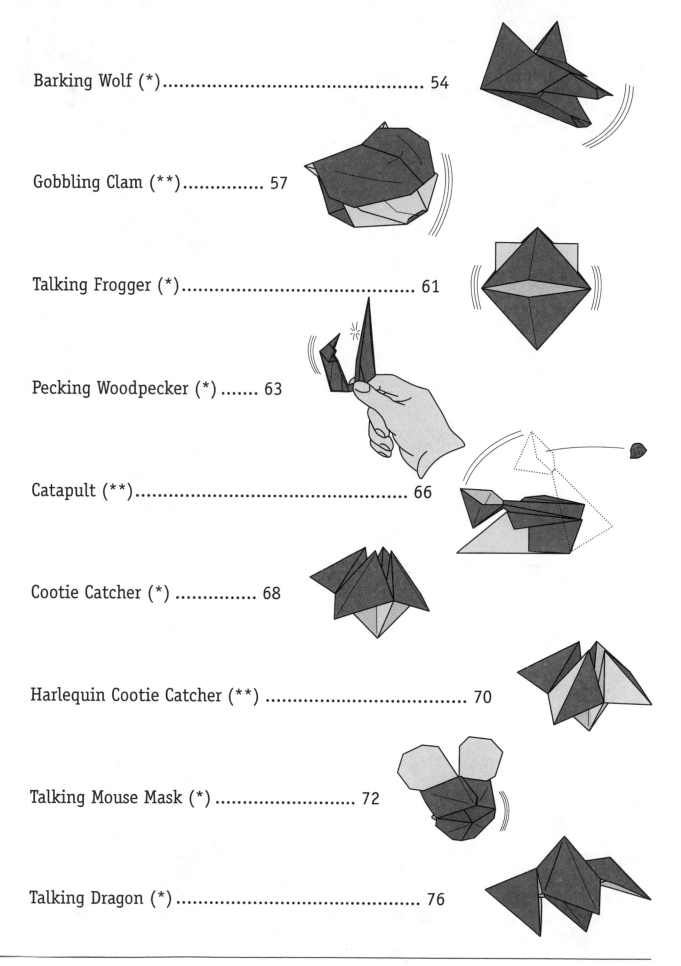

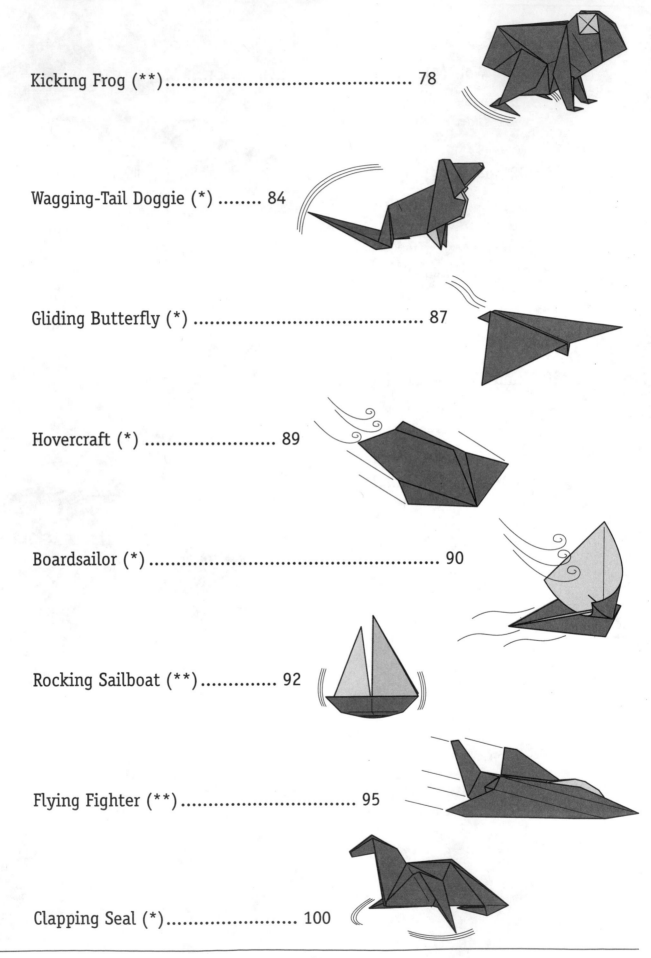

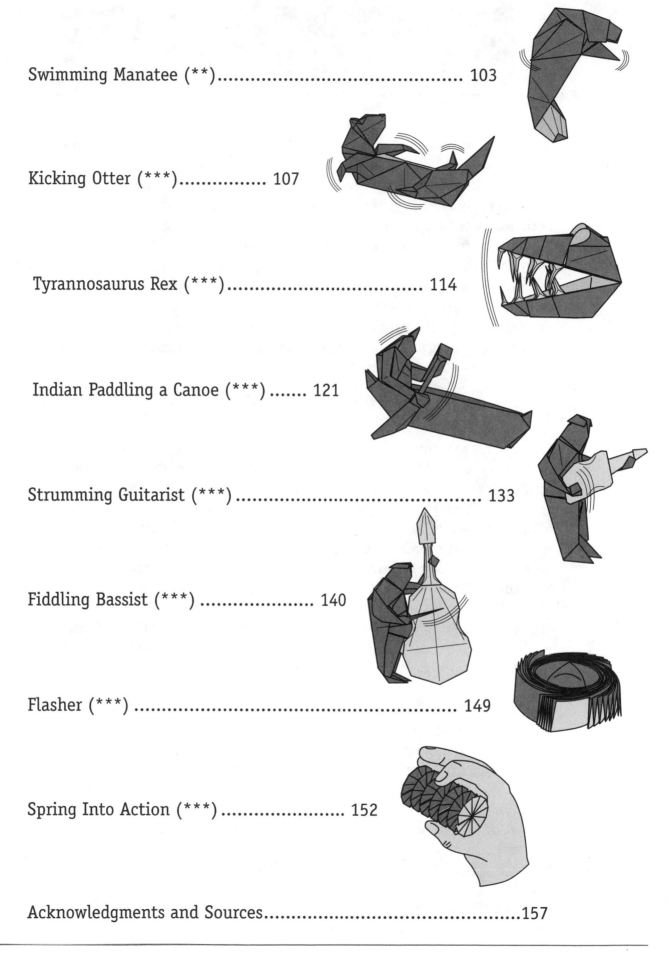

Introduction

In the great pecking order of social skills that prevails in the modern schoolyard, the abilities that elicit good grades run a distant second to the ability to fold cool paper toys from leftover homework. Since time immemorial, paper toys have held a special appeal to the young in age and young at heart — an appeal dating back, perhaps, to the days when primitive man sat around the fire folding flapping pterodactyls from cast-off bits of mammoth skin. Paper has proved a more tractable medium than mammoth hide, and paper airplanes have replaced pterodactyls as the all-purpose toy. Some toys are universal: Everyone knows how to make a dart or glider, it seems (and everyone has his or her own secret tweak for getting the longest flight), but paper airplanes are not the only folds on the fields of Eton. Hot on the contrails of paper airplanes comes the Cootie Catcher (or for the polite among us, the "fortune-teller"), its cousin the talking dragon, and the water-filled paper balloon, ideally suited for dropping on the unwary from second-story windows.

If you don't recognize any of these items from your own younger days, it could be that (1) as a youngster, you were culturally deprived of the finer things in life, or (2) you are still experiencing your younger days and you simply haven't learned them yet. In either case, your salvation is at hand! It is an essential part of growing up — or if you've already grown up, an essential part of growing old — to impress your friends and relatives with the ability to make a talking dragon, a flapping bird, or a working catapult. If you long for this arcane knowledge and the fun — and yes, *status* — it brings, then this book is for you!

This book contains instructions for folding toys from uncut paper — and that's *all* you need. No glue, no scissors, no ruler, no tape. Just you and a sheet of paper, and maybe a surface to fold on. Half of the appeal of folded paper toys is that you can make them *anywhere*. The raw ingredients for paper toys are all around us in the form of letter paper, junk mail, gift wrap, magazines, and of course, the old standby, leftover homework. And where would that paper go if it were not folded into barking dogs? Recent scientific studies have shown that 30% of American landfills consists of discarded paper goods. Thus, recycling used paper into Cootie Catchers is not only fun and entertaining; it's ecologically sound, too!

The art of folding shapes from an uncut sheet of paper is called *origami*, which is a Japanese word meaning "folded paper." Origami is an art that has been around for several hundred years, and there are some pretty snazzy origami models out there: birds, fish, flowers, dinosaurs, cuckoo clocks, and more. Most origami is designed for looks, but the origami in *this* book is designed for *action*. Everything moves: fish swim, otters kick, birds flap. This book contains step-by-step instructions for 38 action origami models, including traditional favorites such as the Cootie Catcher and Waterbomb, as well as some modern novelties: a strumming guitar player, for example, and a toothy Tyrannosaurus Rex. You'll find fish to blow up and cubes that inflate, manatees that swim, and animals that talk. And of course, no collection of action origami would be complete without at least one paper airplane. I've included most of the simple traditional action models plus some far-out creations that will challenge your dexterity and dazzle your peers. Simply follow the step-by-step instructions, and you'll be on your way to the pinnacle of the social pyramid, as your friends gather 'round and utter that most wonderful of phrases:

"Cool! Can you show me how to do that?"

You can, and you will. Read on.

Read This Even If You're a Person Who Never Reads Instructions

The action models in this book cover all levels of difficulty, so if you don't want to be bothered with a bunch of terms and definitions, you can skip the next section, pick one of the easy models (they're the short ones) and dive on in. All you really need to know is that dotted lines show where creases go; black arrows show where the paper goes; and white arrows mean "push here." That much knowledge and a bit of elbow grease will get you through most of the easy models.

However, for the harder models (or if you get stuck on an easy one), it might be worthwhile to come back and visit this section, which defines all of the terms you'll need to know. For all the instructions, I have used the notation and terminology of modern origami, which permits concise, unambiguous description of the folding sequence — at least, in theory! Most origami terms are self-evident: A valley fold is shaped like a valley; a mountain fold is shaped like a mountain. But some of the more complex procedures are not so obvious from their names (a sink fold has nothing to do with plumbing). When you try one of the harder models — or, as I said, if you get stuck on an easy one — come back and read through this section, which defines all of the terms and gives examples of their use.

How To Make a Square from a Rectangle

Everything in this book is folded from a single sheet of paper, but most things are folded from a *square* sheet, and most paper is not square. It's traditional in origami to use a square, so most of the good action models require one. If you are using leftover homework for your folding (ordinary letter paper will do, too) then you need to cut it to a square before you start. Here's how you do it:

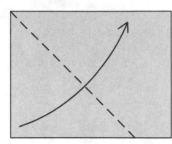

1. Begin with the rectangle oriented horizontally. Fold the bottom left corner up to lie along the top edge, so that the edges line up all the way to the corner.

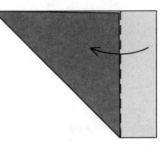

2. Fold the extra strip of paper over on top of the triangle.

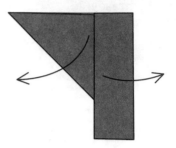

3. Unfold the paper completely.

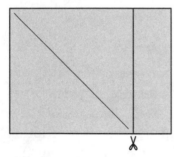

4. Cut along the vertical crease.

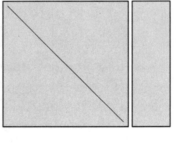

5. The left piece is the desired square.

Here are a couple of tips: If you're making the cut with scissors, flatten the crease completely before you start cutting, or the cut will tend to waver off of the line. If you're using a knife, leave the right side folded over and slide the knife up the crease (as if you were opening a letter with a letter-opener). If you don't have a knife or scissors, you can get a fairly neat rip if you fold the strip back and forth several times to weaken the paper. And finally, if you are doing this in a location where you don't want to make a lot of noise (like algebra class or church), lick your finger and run it along the folded edge before you rip — by dampening the paper, it will rip easily and quietly.

Incidentally, I'll always draw the paper as if it had a colored side and a white side, as above, but you can use paper colored the same on both sides for all models except the Harlequin Cootie Catcher, which loses something if you make it from monotone paper.

Origami Terms

The instructions in this book — and origami instructions in general — combine words and pictures, and if the world were perfect, either one alone would be sufficient. Alas, the world is not perfect and neither are origami diagrams. You'll have the best luck folding if you look at each step AND read the words underneath each step before you start folding.

When you're folding, you should keep your paper in the same orientation as the picture on the page, because all of the directions will be given with respect to the page. So, for example, "the bottom point" means, "the point on your model that corresponds to the point in the picture closest to the bottom of the page." You might actually be more comfortable turning your paper sideways or upside-down to make the fold; just make sure you turn it back to the orientation of the picture when you're done, or Bad Things will happen in the next step.

So, in verbal directions, "top," "bottom," "left," and "right" are defined with respect to the page. The layers closest to you (what you might call the "top layer" in casual conversation, but we're already using "top" to mean something else) are called the "near layers"; those farthest are called the "far layers."

We'll also make a distinction between "crease" and "fold." A crease is a mark on the paper left by a previous fold that was undone; a fold is a fold that stays put. Similarly, when we say to "crease the paper," we mean to fold the paper and unfold it, leaving a crease behind. These terms and others are illustrated below.

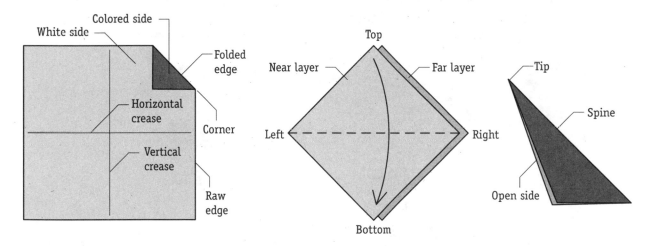

There are only two ways that a fold can go — forward and backward, and we call them valley and mountain folds, respectively. Valley folds are denoted with a dashed line; mountain folds are denoted with a dot-dot-dash line; creases are denoted by a thin line; and stuff that's hidden from view is denoted with a dotted, or x-ray, line. The figure on the next page shows all the lines in origami. You can cut it out and keep it in your wallet with your credit cards for ready reference.

Valley fold =
fold the paper
toward you

X-ray line =
hidden edge or
crease

Mountain fold =
fold the paper
behind

Crease =
location of an
earlier fold,
since unfolded

Push here

Turn the paper over

Rotate the paper

View from this vantage point

Repeat a range of steps

23–24

Right angle

This next section goes through all of the basic procedures of origami that are used in this book. You can read through it all if you want to be fully prepared for anything, or you can read just the easy stuff, then go have some fun and fold some toys before you come back to the harder procedures. Take your pick.

Really Easy Folds

Origami models are made by stringing together groups of simple folds. In the easiest models, you only make one fold at a time. The simplest folds are shown here. Just to get used to following the drawings, you might want to take a sheet of paper and try all the simple steps shown here.

Valley Fold

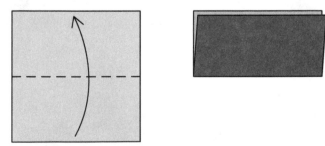

A valley fold is what we call a fold in which the moving part of the paper comes toward you. It is the most common type of fold, so we frequently leave off the word "valley" and just say something like, "fold the bottom of the paper up to the top." A valley fold is always indicated by a dashed line.

Mountain Fold

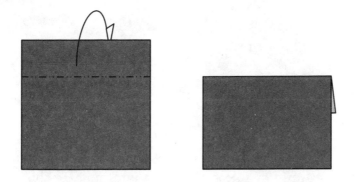

A mountain fold is what we call a fold in which the moving part goes away from you. You can often make a mountain fold by turning the paper over and making a valley fold, then turning it back over. I could have shown them this way, but instead of using lots of turn-over arrows and drawing lots of extra steps, I'll just show a mountain fold line and leave all the turning-over to you. More complicated procedures have both valley and mountain folds in them, so turning the paper wouldn't work on those anyhow! A mountain fold is always indicated by a dot-dot-dash line. I also use a single-sided arrowhead to show the motion of the paper.

Unfold

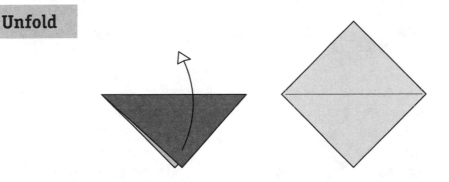

This one's an easy fold to make! Sometimes you'll unfold the paper because you just want to leave a crease behind as a reference mark. (Sometimes you'll also unfold it because you did something wrong and need to start over, but you won't find that in the instructions.) I'll use a hollow arrow to indicate when you are unfolding something. (Compare this to the arrows used with valley and mountain folds.) I'll also use this arrow to indicate when you are pulling some paper out of a pocket as shown below.

Fold and Unfold

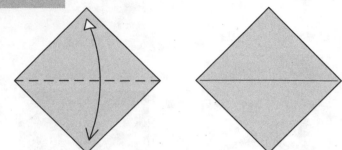

 If you are making a crease just to get a reference mark, sometimes I'll combine the "fold" and the "unfold" into a single step; to indicate this on the drawing, I combine the arrows for folding and unfolding into a single arrow as shown above. You can also think of this arrow as saying, "bring the two points at each end of the arrow together, crease, and unfold." Here's a tip: Quite often, you don't need the entire crease to use as a reference mark. If you see from the next step about where the reference point will be, then you can make the crease sharp just where it's needed and avoid cluttering up the rest of the paper with unnecessary creases.

Okay, those are the basics of origami! If you want to take a break, go fold the cootie catcher or dragon, which only require valley and mountain folds. Then come on back here and we'll go through some slightly harder stuff.

Not-Quite-As-Easy Folds

If only all origami consisted of nothing but simple valley and mountain folds! Unfortunately, sometimes you have to do more complicated stuff, like turning a flap inside-out, or bringing together several creases at once. In each of the procedures shown in this section, you have to make several creases happen together. These procedures are common throughout origami, so when you learn them, you'll be ready to tackle most of the folds in this book. It's a good idea to practice making the simple examples shown here before you go on to the more complicated models.

Inside Reverse Fold

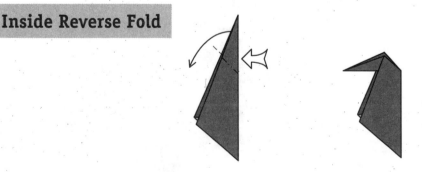

A reverse fold is a way of simultaneously turning a point inside-out and changing its direction. You can use a valley or mountain fold to change its direction, but a reverse fold is more permanent. Actually, it's a half-and-half mixture, since in an inside reverse fold, the near layers get mountain-folded and the far layers get valley-folded. The inside reverse fold is indicated by a push arrow. You turn the point being folded inside-out and push it between the layers of the rest of the flap.

Here's a tip for making a clean reverse fold: First valley-fold the point so that it points in the direction you want the final reverse fold to go. Then unfold and mountain-fold the point away from you along the same crease line and unfold. Now when you make the reverse fold, the paper will naturally fall into place once you've turned the tip inside-out. Try it, you'll see.

Outside Reverse Fold

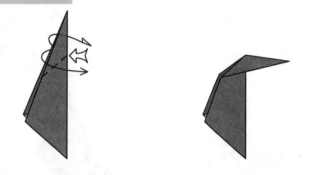

The outside reverse fold is very much like the inside reverse fold, but it goes the opposite direction. In the outside reverse fold, the valley fold is on the near layer; the mountain fold is on the far layer. It's also a bit harder to make.

Here's a tip for making a clean outside reverse fold: Precrease the flap (by folding it to lie along its final direction and unfolding) on both sides of the paper. Then open the edges of the paper and simultaneously press your thumb against the base of the fold (where the hollow "push" arrow is above) and "pop" the top of the flap inside-out. As you close the model and flatten it, the creases will tend to fall into place.

Rabbit Ear Fold

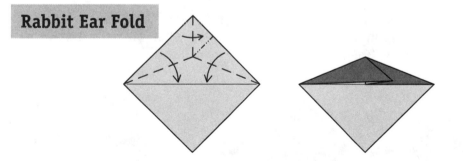

A rabbit ear looks complicated because four creases have to come together at once! (Usually it's three valley folds and a mountain fold.) There is a secret to making a perfect rabbit ear every time: If you get the valley folds right, the mountain fold forms naturally in the right place when you flatten the paper. A rabbit ear is usually made on a triangular flap. You pinch the corners of the triangle in half to make the valley folds and through the wonders of Euclidean geometry, the three folds always meet at a single point. (If they don't, that's usually a tip-off that you've done something wrong.) Swing the excess paper to one side and flatten. Voilà! the completed rabbit ear.

Squash Fold

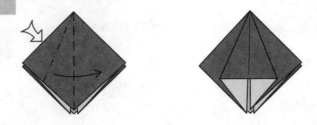

A squash fold is a way of flattening a flap that has a pocket. To make it, you stand the flap up so that it pokes out at you, spread the edges of the pocket, and then squash it flat (this can be very satisfying when you are frustrated). Usually, it's made symmetrically, so the crease that used to be an edge winds up centered, as shown in the example above.

Petal Fold

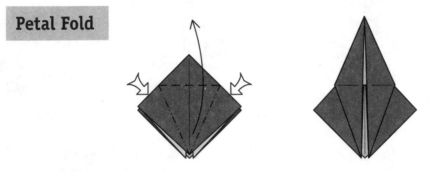

The petal fold is a very important procedure because it is the basis of the granddaddy of all action figures, the traditional Japanese flapping bird. A petal fold is a way of narrowing a point that actually makes it longer. It is shown here as it occurs in the flapping bird. As you lift up the point, you push in the sides, which ultimately meet in the middle of the flap. Like reverse folds, petal folds are a lot easier if you do some precreasing.

As you get more practice at making petal folds, you'll learn how to make them without precreasing (which is more accurate); however, when you're just starting out, they are a lot easier if you precrease as shown below.

1. The most common petal fold starts with this shape, called the Preliminary Fold. See the Traditional Flapping Bird for an example.

2. Fold the sides in to lie along the center line.

3. Fold the top point down over the other two flaps.

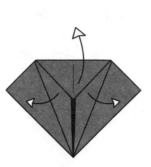 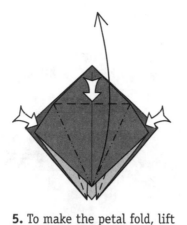 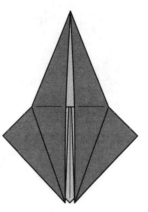

4. Unfold all three flaps.

5. To make the petal fold, lift up the first layer of the bottom corner while holding down the top of the model just above the horizontal crease. Allow the sides to swing in.

6. Finished petal fold.

Most of the time a petal fold is performed on a corner of the paper. However, it's also possible to create a corner from an edge by petal-folding, as shown here.

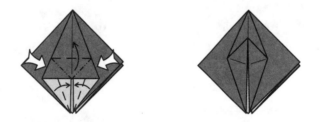

When you petal-fold an edge, you can't easily precrease the mountain folds, which makes it a little bit harder.

Crimps and Pleats

The thing that transforms a plain vanilla flap of paper into a head, wing, leg, or arm is often a set of two or more zig-zag folds that shorten the flap, change its direction, or add a line or two running across it to define a joint. These folds are known collectively as crimps and pleats. There is some disagreement in the origami world as to precisely what is a crimp and what is a pleat. In this book, the term "pleat" will be used to describe the situation when all of the layers of a flap are folded together, as shown below.

It's hard to show all of the layers in a crimp or pleat (some pleats have ten or twenty layers) so I'll usually draw a set of zig-zag lines next to the pleat (as above) that show how the edges are arranged (as if you were looking at the pleat edge-on). Pleats are easy to make; you just fold the flap one way, then fold it back the other.

Crimps are a different story. It's a crimp when the paper goes inside itself, as shown below. You can sometimes make a crimp by unfolding the paper and making a pleat before re-folding it; other times, you have no recourse but to make two sequential reverse-folds. Note the difference between the edge view of a crimp (below) and a pleat (above).

Congratulations! If you've made examples of all the steps above, you can fold most of the models in this book, and for that matter, most of the origami models in the world. If you want to fold the most challenging models (which are also the ones that inspire the most awe in your audience), you will need to master a few more difficult procedures, all of which are called "sink folds."

Definitely-Not-Easy Folds

Okay, you say, Cootie Catchers are for kids and flapping fowl are for the birds. What you want to make are the toughies — the guitarist, bass player, or paddling Indian. Those (and others) are fairly difficult folds and you should practice on some of the easy ones first. Then gird yourself for battle, read through the next couple of folds, and have at 'em.

Spread Sink Fold

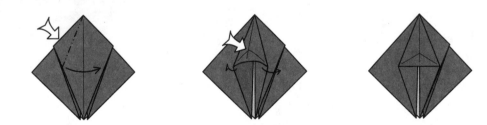

Sink folds comprise a way of inverting a point when there are no raw edges around to ease your burden (otherwise, a simple reverse fold would do the trick). The simplest and easiest sink fold is the spread sink, which practically folds itself. The spread sink is similar to a squash fold; you open out two edges of the point to be sunk and stretch them as far apart as possible. As you do this, the point flattens out and disappears.

Open Sink Fold

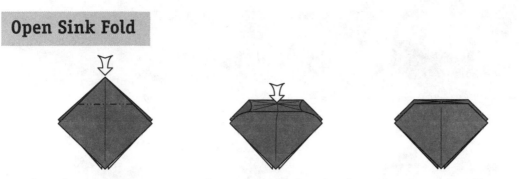

Rather than opening out a point, you can also simply make the point disappear. One way to do this is the open sink, in which the paper is flattened completely during the inversion process. Here's a tip on making an open sink: Pre-crease along the line of the sink, then open out the point and pinch a mountain fold all the way around the polygon that defines the sink (it's a square in the example above). If you then push down the middle and flatten the paper, the creases inside the model practically fall into place by themselves. And even if they don't, since they're hidden inside, no one's going to see them anyhow.

Closed Sink Fold

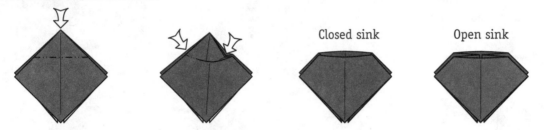

Closed sink   Open sink

The toughest maneuver in the standard origami repertoire is the closed sink, which inverts a point without opening it out flat. One way to do a closed sink is to open out the bottom of the point to be sunk, making the point conical (after precreasing — you should always precrease a closed sink!) and then "pop" the corner inside out, starting near the base of the cone. Compare the two above; the edges of the closed sink are locked together.

If the point to be sunk is very sharp, it's almost impossible to invert it directly. Here's a way to cheat: Fold a rabbit ear from the point, then bring one layer in front of the rabbit ear. This is easier since the corner of the rabbit ear is blunt. Then carefully push down all the layers of the rabbit ear inside the newly formed pocket.

What's Next

What, you're still here? You should be folding something! Turn the page and get started!

Traditional Flapping Bird

Traditional design

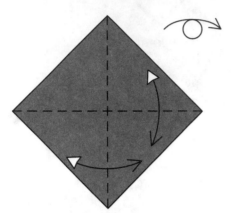

1. Begin with the colored side up. Fold the paper in half along the diagonals and unfold. Turn the paper over.

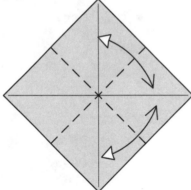

2. Fold and unfold by bringing one edge to the opposite edge. Do this in both directions.

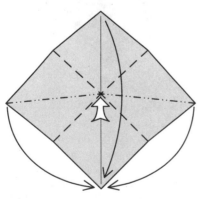

3. Push in the center and bring all four corners together at the bottom.

4. Flatten the paper. This is called a Preliminary Fold.

5. Fold the sides of the front flaps in to the center line and unfold.

 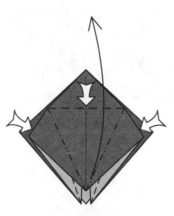  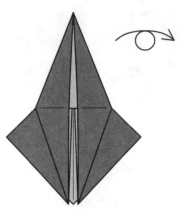

6. Fold the top point down and unfold.

7. Petal-fold the flap upward. To do this, lift up one corner while holding down the top of the model just above the horizontal crease and let the sides swing in.

8. Bring the side edges in to meet in the middle and flatten the top point upward.

9. Turn the model over.

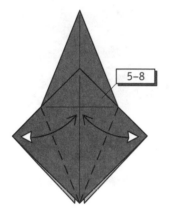 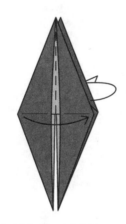 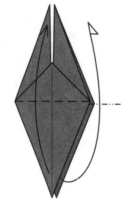 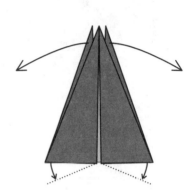

10. Repeat steps 5–8 on this side.

11. This is a Bird Base. Fold one flap to the right in front and one to the left behind.

12. Fold one flap up in front and one up behind.

13. Pull the two middle points out to the sides and flatten them at their base.

14. Reverse-fold the point downward.

15. Put your finger in the pocket and curl the wing to the right. Repeat behind.

16. Finished Traditional Flapping Bird. Hold the neck and tail and pull the tail in the direction of the arrow. The wings will flap.

Randlett's Flapping Bird

Designed by Samuel L. Randlett

This flapping bird is nearly foolproof to operate. The basic mechanism can be used in many other action figures. Begin with a square of paper 6 to 10 inches across, colored side up.

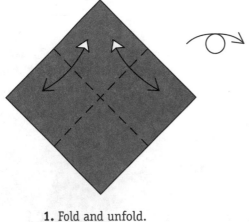

1. Fold and unfold. Turn the paper over.

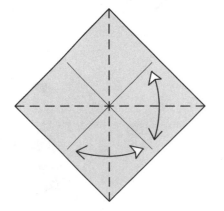

2. Fold and unfold.

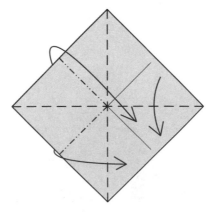

3. Fold the sides in and collapse the paper.

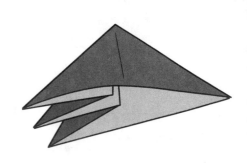

4. Flatten.

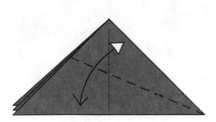

5. Fold and unfold through all layers.

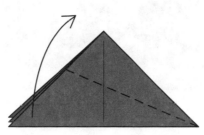

6. Fold the nearest of the three flaps on the left upward.

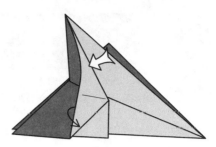

7. Flatten the excess paper in the gusset downward.

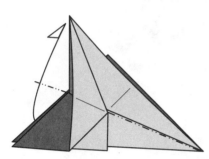

8. Repeat steps 6–7 behind.

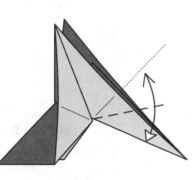

9. Fold and unfold.

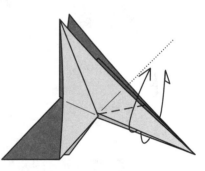

10. Wrap the bottom layers up and around, so that you turn the white point inside-out. Flatten on the creases you just made.

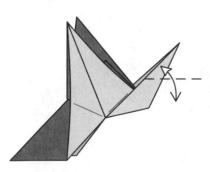

11. Fold and unfold.

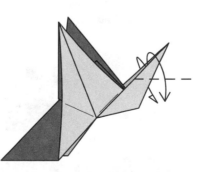

12. Wrap the top layers around and turn the tip of the white point inside-out. Flatten on the creases you just made.

13. Finished Randlett's Flapping Bird. Hold at the base of the neck and tail and pull; the bird will flap its wings.

Flapping Butterfly

Designed by deg farelly

For a butterfly that fits your finger, use a 3 to 4 inch square.

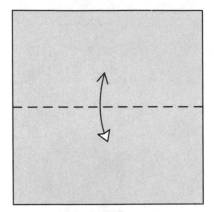

1. Fold the the bottom of the square up to the top and unfold.

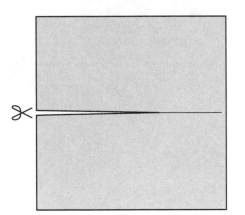

2. Cut the square into two rectangles. You can fold one butterfly from each half.

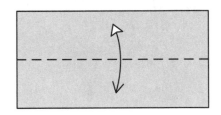

3. With the white side facing up, fold the rectangle in half the long way and unfold.

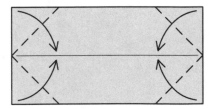

4. Fold all four corners in to lie along the horizontal center line.

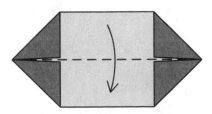

5. Fold the model in half.

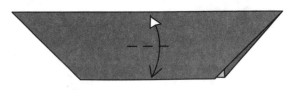

6. Fold both raw edges up to the top folded edge and make a short valley pinch through both layers at the center. Do not crease the entire length of the model.

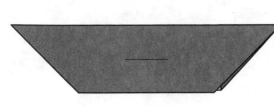

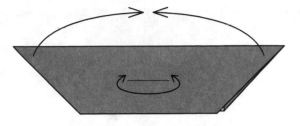

7. Turn the model over.

8. Bring the wing tips together so that the valley crease (made in step 6) is on the outside. Form a loose loop from the paper; do not crease.

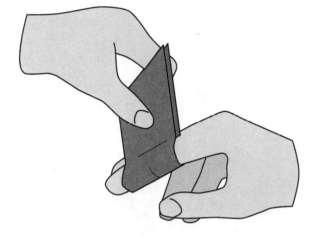

9. Insert your index finger into the loop while holding the wing tips together. Slide the fingers of your other hand down to form the body of the butterfly snugly around your finger.

10. Reinforce the dent in the center of the model evenly along the valley fold you made in step 6.

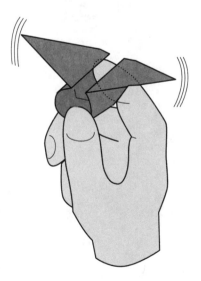

11. Like this.

12. Finished Flapping Butterfly. Insert a finger and thumb into each side of the body and pinch the fingers together to make the butterfly flap its wings.

Intermediate Flapping Butterfly

Designed by deg farelly

This variation of the Flapping Butterfly has swallowtails on its wings. You might enjoy trying to come up with variations of your own with other shapes or patterns on the wings. Use a 3 to 4 inch square.

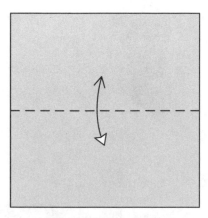

1. Begin with the white side facing up. Fold the bottom edge up to the top and unfold.

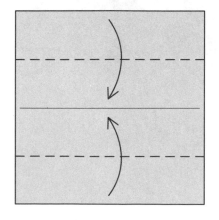

2. Fold the top and bottom edges to lie along the center line.

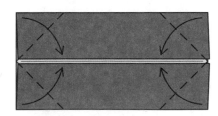

3. Fold four corners to the center line.

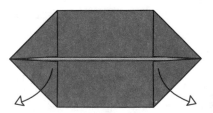

4. Unfold the lower two corners.

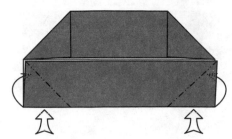

5. Reverse-fold the two bottom corners inside using the existing creases.

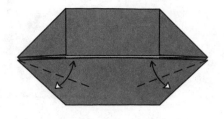

6. Bring the diagonal edge to the center line, crease lightly, and unfold.

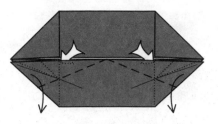

7. Twist each corner downward and squash the hidden layers, using the crease you just made.

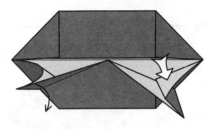

8. This shows the twist in progress on the left and a little further along on the right.

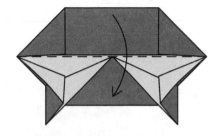

9. Fold the top half down over the bottom.

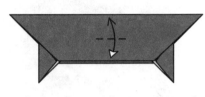

10. Continue with steps 6–12 of the Butterfly.

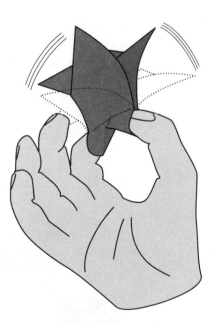

11. Finished Intermediate Flapping Butterfly.

Flapping Eagle

Designed by Robert J. Lang

Use a square of paper 6 to 12 inches. Begin with the colored side up to get a white head and a colored body.

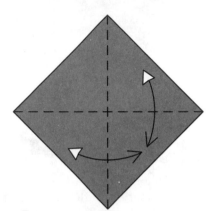

1. Begin with the colored side up. Fold and unfold along the diagonals.

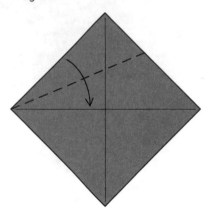

2. Fold one edge down to the diagonal.

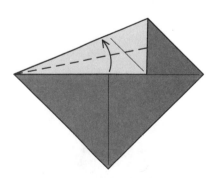

3. Fold the raw edge back up to the folded edge.

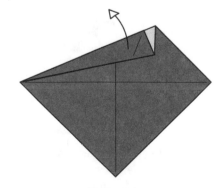

4. Unfold.

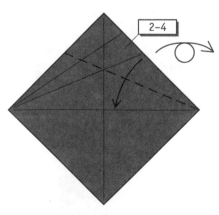

2-4

5. Repeat steps 2–4 on the right. Then turn the paper over.

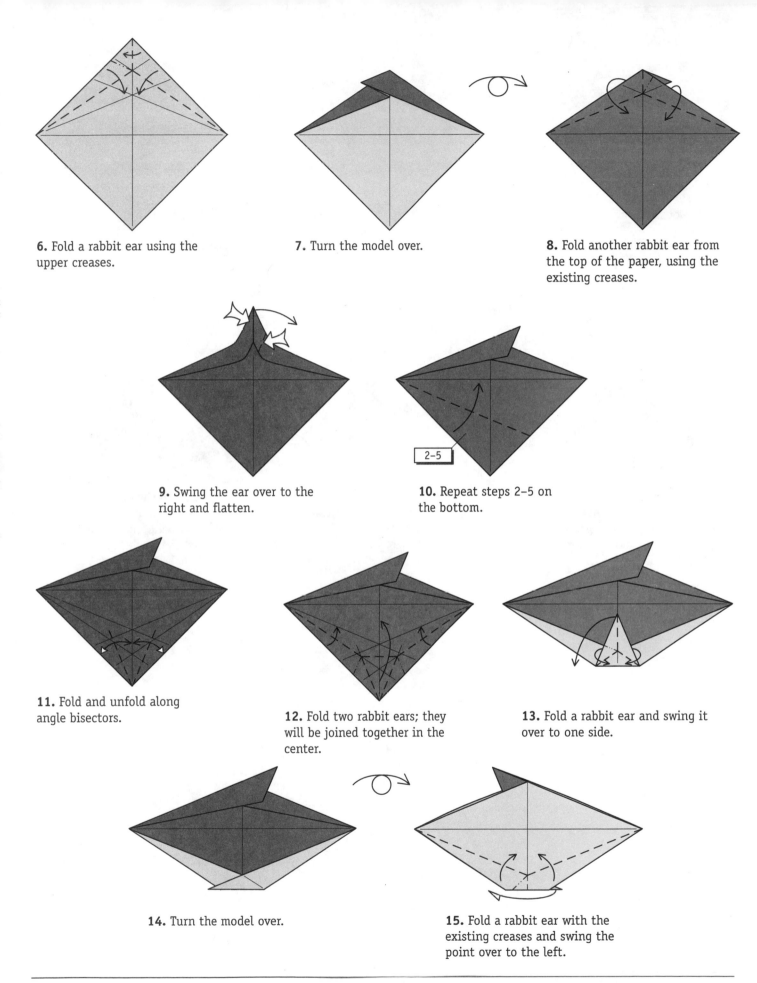

6. Fold a rabbit ear using the upper creases.

7. Turn the model over.

8. Fold another rabbit ear from the top of the paper, using the existing creases.

9. Swing the ear over to the right and flatten.

10. Repeat steps 2–5 on the bottom.

2–5

11. Fold and unfold along angle bisectors.

12. Fold two rabbit ears; they will be joined together in the center.

13. Fold a rabbit ear and swing it over to one side.

14. Turn the model over.

15. Fold a rabbit ear with the existing creases and swing the point over to the left.

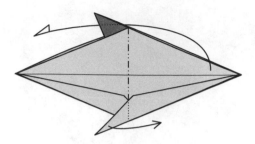

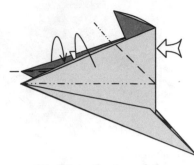

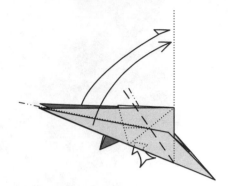

16. Mountain-fold the right side behind.

17. Crimp the top of the model downward and to the left.

18. Fold one wing upward, squash-folding the hidden edge underneath. Repeat behind.

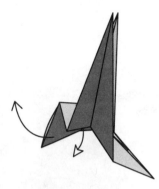

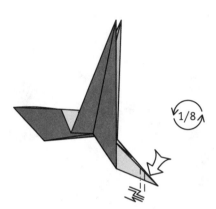

19. Rotate the bottom point clockwise and pull as much paper as possible out of the model. Flatten the paper near the front of the tail.

20. Crimp the top point. Two layers go one way and one goes the other. Rotate the model 1/4 turn counterclockwise.

21. Finished Flapping Eagle. Hold at the circles and pull, and the eagle will flap its wings.

Flapping Duck

Designed by Robert J. Lang

The Traditional Flapping Bird (p. 18) can easily be turned into many different types of birds by altering the head and tail. This modification removes the pyramid in the middle of the back, which has the side effect of giving a very duck-like flapping action. Use a square of paper 10 to 12 inches.

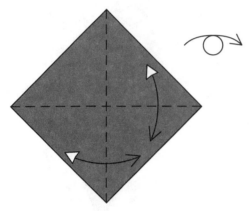

1. Begin with the colored side up. Fold the paper in half along the diagonals and unfold. Turn the paper over.

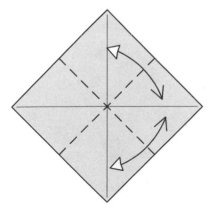

2. Fold and unfold by bringing one edge to the opposite edge. Do this in both directions.

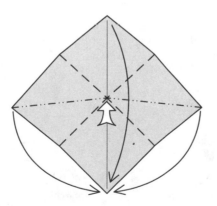

3. Push in the center and bring all four corners together at the bottom.

4. Flatten the paper into a Preliminary Fold.

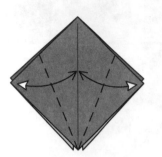

5. Fold the sides of the front flaps in to the center line and unfold.

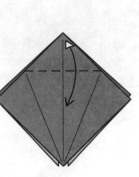

6. Fold the top point down and unfold.

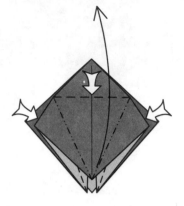

7. Petal-fold the flap upward. To do this, lift up one corner while holding down the top of the model just above the horizontal crease and let the sides swing in.

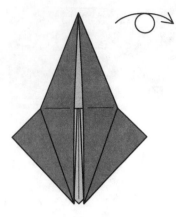

8. Turn the model over.

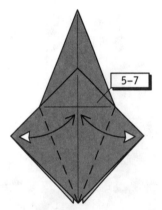

9. Repeat steps 5–7 on this side.

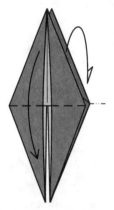

10. This is a Bird Base. Fold one flap down in front. Repeat behind.

11. Fold the top point down to the horizontal crease; crease firmly and unfold.

12. Sink the top point on the creases you just made. Steps 13–14 show how to do this.

13. Pull the two near layers toward you and simultaneously push down on the top point so that it flattens out into a small square, outlined by creases all the way around.

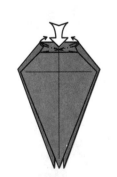

14. Push the middle down inside and flatten the model.

15. Fold two edges together to the center line; crease firmly and unfold.

16. Pull out two raw edges.

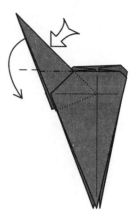

17. Reverse-fold in and out on the existing creases.

18. Reverse-fold both sets of raw edges.

19. Reverse-fold one point upward so that the left edges line up.

20. Reverse-fold the point downward.

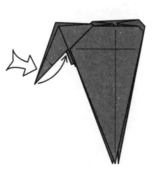

21. Fold and unfold.

22. Outside reverse-fold the point using the creases you just made.

23. Fold the corner to the right. Repeat behind.

24. Fold the near and far layers downward.

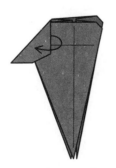

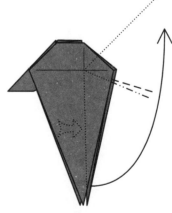

25. Bring one layer in front. Repeat behind.

26. Mountain-fold two corners inside.

27. Reverse-fold the middle point upward.

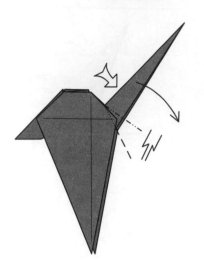

28. Crimp the long point downward, tucking the corners inside.

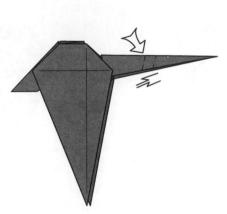

29. Crimp the neck to form a head.

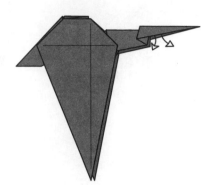

30. Pull out all layers of paper.

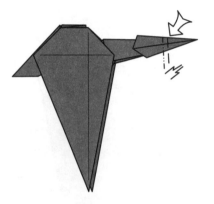

31. Crimp the beak.

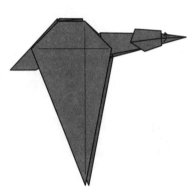

32. Lift up one raw edge on each side of the beak to change its color.

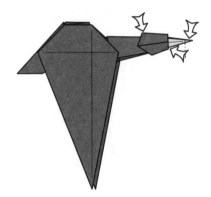

33. Round the head by reverse-folding the corners and the tip of the beak.

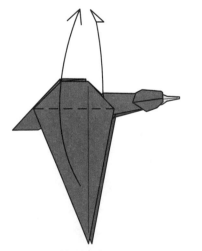

34. Lift up the wings, one on each side.

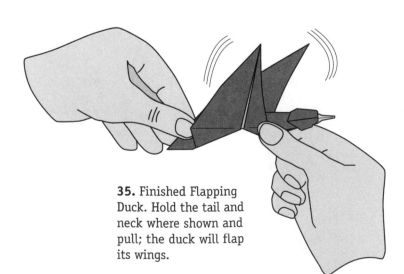

35. Finished Flapping Duck. Hold the tail and neck where shown and pull; the duck will flap its wings.

Flapping Crane

Designed by Robert J. Lang

This model combines the action mechanism of the Traditional Flapping Bird with John Montroll's "Five-Sided Square" to complete a Crane. This is a somewhat difficult model; use a 10 to 12 inch square for your first attempt.

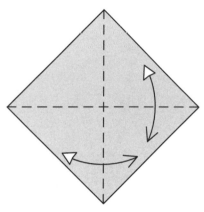

1. Begin with the white side up for a white bird with colored legs. Fold the paper in half along the diagonals and unfold.

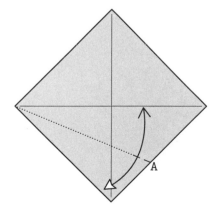

2. Fold the lower left edge up to the horizontal crease and pinch at the right edge; unfold. This creates point A.

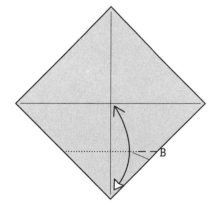

3. Fold the bottom point up to touch the center of the square, making the crease sharp only where it hits the right edge. Unfold. This creates point B.

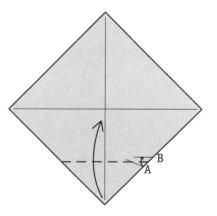

4. Fold the bottom point up so that point A lies on the crease you just made (which is connected to point B).

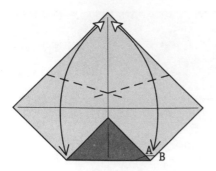

5. Fold the top point down to touch each of the two bottom corners, crease from the center out to the edges, and unfold.

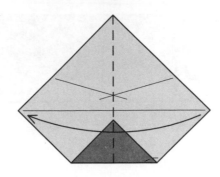

6. Fold the paper in half vertically.

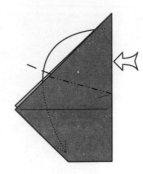

7. Reverse-fold the top corner on the existing creases.

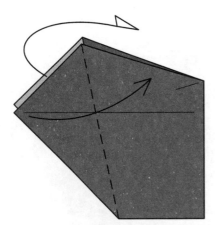

8. Fold one flap to the right in front and one to the left behind.

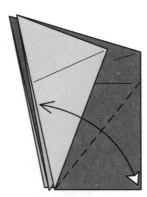

9. Fold the bottom edge up to lie along the left edge and unfold.

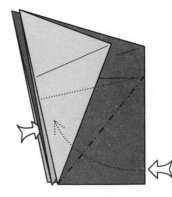

10. Reverse-fold the right edge on the crease you just made. Put the edge behind the middle layer.

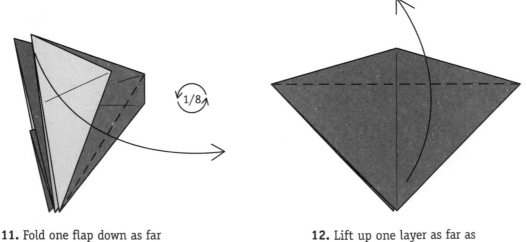

11. Fold one flap down as far as it will go. Rotate the model about 1/8 turn counterclockwise.

12. Lift up one layer as far as possible.

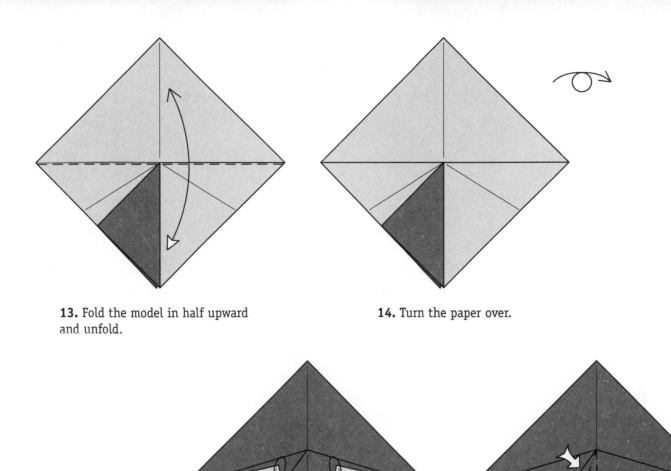

13. Fold the model in half upward and unfold.

14. Turn the paper over.

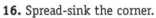

15. Mountain-fold the corners on the creases you just made.

16. Spread-sink the corner.

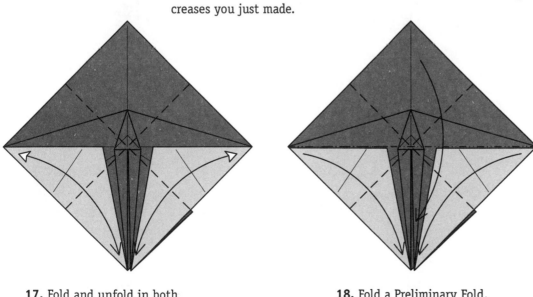

17. Fold and unfold in both directions, folding through all layers.

18. Fold a Preliminary Fold.

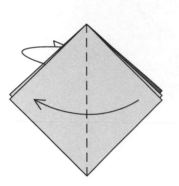

19. Fold one flap to the left in front and one to the right behind.

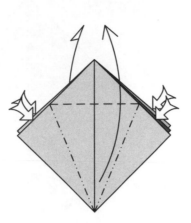

20. Petal-fold the front and back flaps.

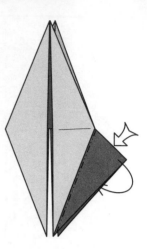

21. Reverse-fold the colored flap inside.

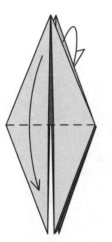

22. Fold the two flaps at the top downward.

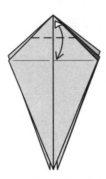

23. Fold and unfold through all layers.

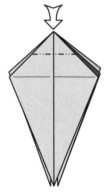

24. Carefully open-sink the five-sided point at the top.

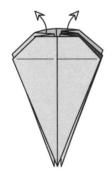

25. Pull out two points from the top.

26. Fold one flap to the left.

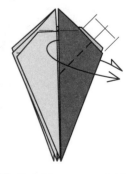

27. Outside reverse-fold the colored layer down.

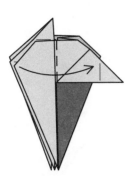 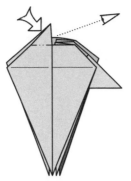 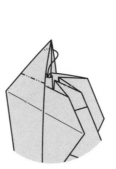 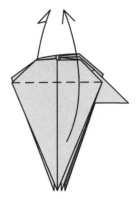

28. Fold one flap back to the right.

29. Reverse-fold the point and tuck it into the pocket. See the next step for details.

30. Close-up view showing the pocket that the point gets tucked into.

31. Fold one flap up in front and behind.

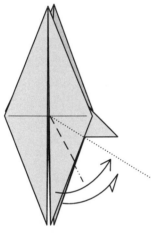 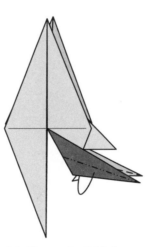 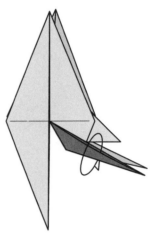

32. Valley-fold one flap to the right in front. Repeat behind.

33. Mountain-fold the edge underneath. Repeat behind.

34. Loosen one layer along the top of the leg and wrap it around the bottom of the leg from front to back. Repeat behind.

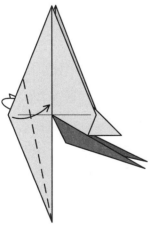 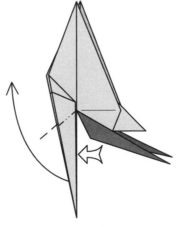 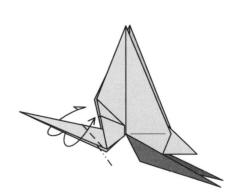

35. Valley-fold one edge to the right. Repeat behind.

36. Reverse-fold the neck up to the left.

37. Outside reverse-fold the neck.

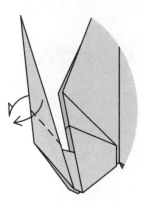
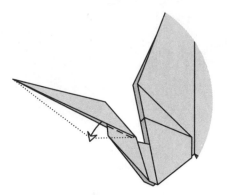
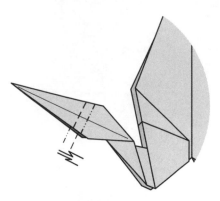

38. Enlarged view of head. Outside reverse-fold the neck again to form a head.

39. Pull out both layers of the loose paper from each side.

40. Crimp the point.

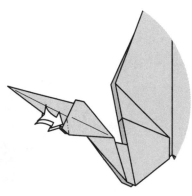
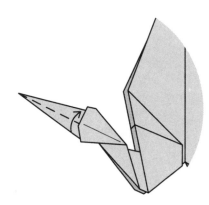

41. Reverse-fold the corners of the face.

42. Valley-fold the near edge upward. Repeat behind.

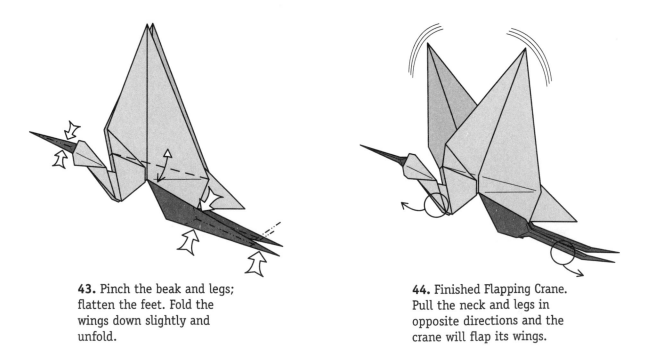

43. Pinch the beak and legs; flatten the feet. Fold the wings down slightly and unfold.

44. Finished Flapping Crane. Pull the neck and legs in opposite directions and the crane will flap its wings.

Flapping Lovebirds

Designed by Robert J. Lang

Randlett's Flapping Bird (p. 20) has always been my favorite of the various flapping birds in the origami literature, because of its simple, clean action. Here are two Randlett birds from a single square, flapping in an avian embrace. Use a ten inch square.

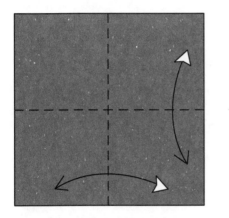

1. Fold the paper in half and unfold. Turn the paper over.

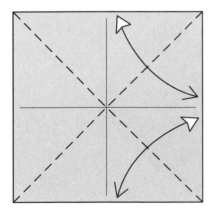

2. Fold and unfold.

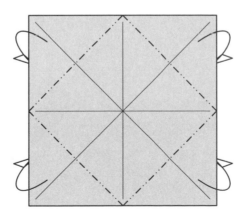

3. Fold four corners behind.

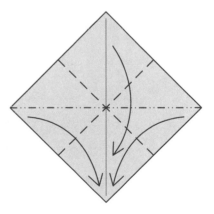

4. Fold a Preliminary Fold.

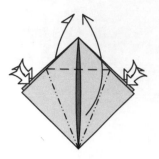 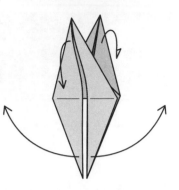 

5. Petal-fold front and back to make a Bird Base.

6. Stretch the two bottom points out to the sides and swing the two top points down. The center "hump" should pop down, forming a long valley or groove along the top of the model.

7. Push in the sides and flatten.

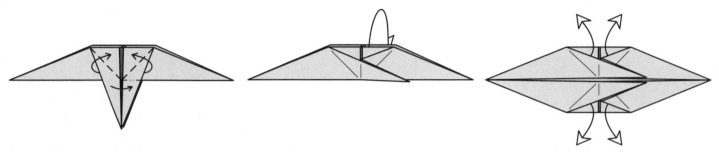

8. Fold a rabbit ear. Repeat behind.

9. Swing the back half of the model downward.

10. Pull out the four loose corners completely out from the back.

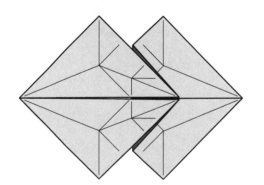 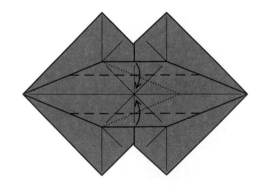

11. Turn the model over from top to bottom.

12. Fold two edges toward the center line as far as possible.

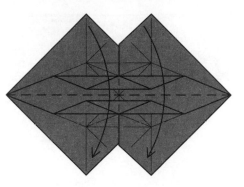

13. Fold the model in half.

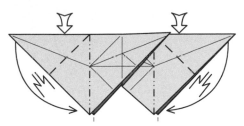

14. Crimp the two ends downward.

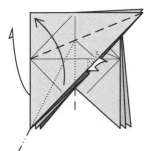

15. Fold the raw edge upward, squash-folding the hidden edge. Repeat behind.

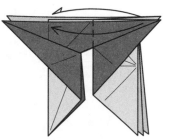

16. Fold a point to the left in front and behind.

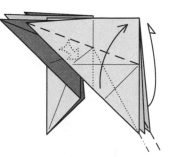

17. Repeat step 15 on the right.

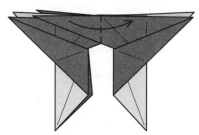

18. Fold one point to the right. Do not repeat behind.

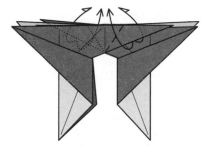

19. Outside reverse-fold the point on each side. Be careful not to rip the paper.

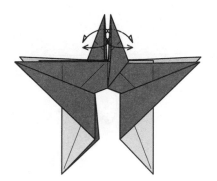

20. Outside reverse-fold each point again. This one is easier.

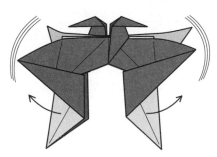

21. Finished Flapping Lovebirds. Pull the tails away from each other; the wings will flap.

Inflatable Waterbomb

Traditional design

The Waterbomb can be made from almost any size paper and, true to its name, will hold water. They're great for dropping out of windows!

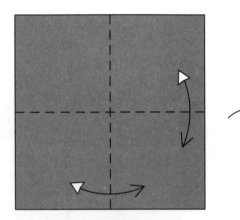

1. Begin with the colored side up. Fold the paper in half vertically and horizontally and unfold. Turn the paper over.

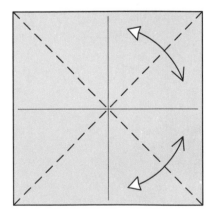

2. Fold the paper in half along both diagonals and unfold.

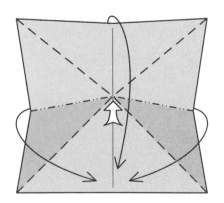

3. Push in the center of the paper and simultaneously bring the middle of three sides to the bottom.

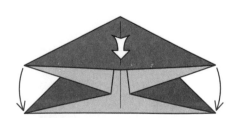

4. Flatten the paper completely, aligning the corners.

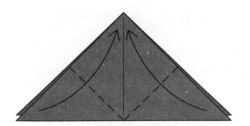

5. Fold the two front corners up to the top of the model.

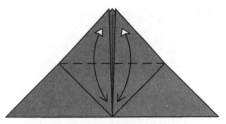

6. Fold the two corners down to the bottom, crease, and unfold.

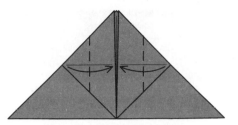

7. Fold the two corners in to meet in the middle of the model.

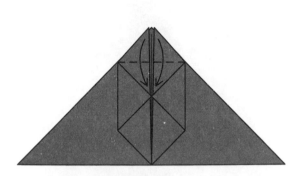

8. Fold the two top corners down to touch the two corners you just folded.

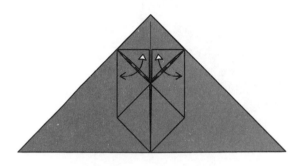

9. Fold the corners out to the sides and unfold.

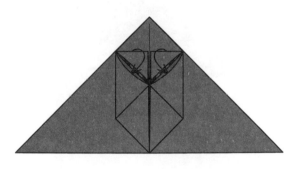

10. Tuck the corners into the pockets.

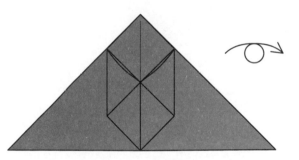

11. Turn the model over.

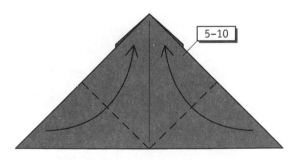

12. Repeat steps 5–10 on this side.

13. Inflate by blowing into the hole in the bottom.

14. Finished Inflatable Waterbomb.

Blow-up Bunny

Traditional Chinese design

Use a 6 to 10 inch square.

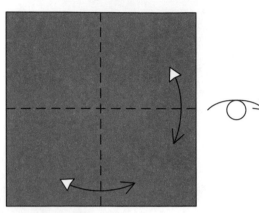

1. Begin with the colored side up. Fold the paper in half vertically and horizontally and unfold. Turn the paper over.

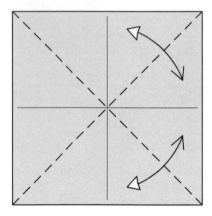

2. Fold the paper in half along both diagonals and unfold.

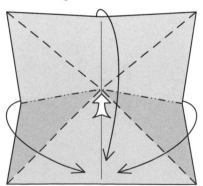

3. Push in the center of the paper and simultaneously bring the middle of three sides to the bottom.

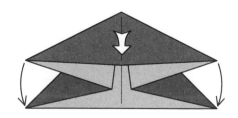

4. Flatten the paper completely, aligning the corners.

5. Fold the near flaps inward so that their edges meet along the center line.

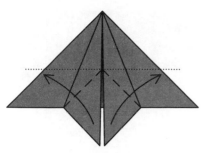

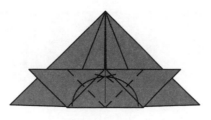

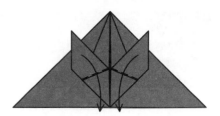

6. Fold the corners up and out to the sides so that their upper edges are horizontal.

7. Fold the bottom edges of the two folded flaps up to meet in the middle.

8. Fold two flaps downward so that their edges meet along the center line.

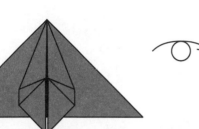

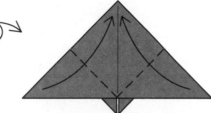

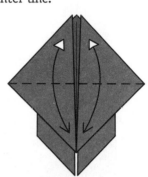

9. Turn the paper over from side to side.

10. Fold the two remaining corners up to the top of the model.

11. Fold the two corners down to the bottom, crease, and unfold.

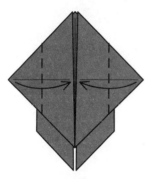

12. Fold the two corners in to meet in the middle of the model.

13. Fold the two top corners down to touch the two corners you just folded.

14. Fold the corners out to the sides and unfold.

15. Tuck the corners into the pockets.

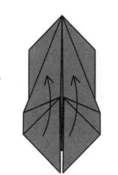

16. Turn the model over.

17. Lift up two flaps.

18. Blow in through the hole in the nose to inflate. For best results, don't inflate completely.

19. Finished Blow-up Bunny.

Sitting Bunny

Designed by Robert J. Lang

It is easy to over-inflate the traditional Blow-up Bunny; this variation is less likely to come apart and has feet in the bargain! Use a 6 to 10 inch square.

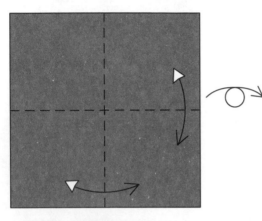

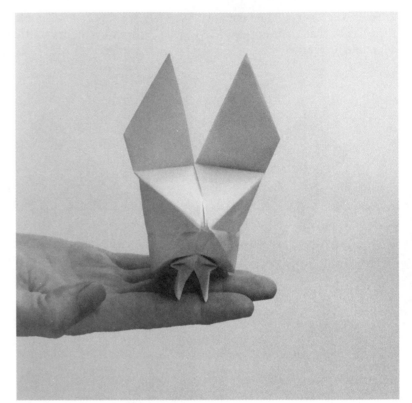

1. Begin with the colored side up. Fold the paper in half vertically and horizontally and unfold. Turn the paper over.

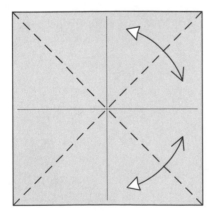

2. Fold the paper in half along both diagonals and unfold.

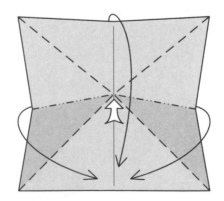

3. Push in the center of the paper and simultaneously bring the middle of three sides to the bottom.

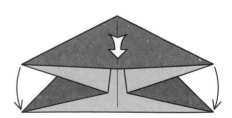

4. Flatten the paper completely, aligning the corners.

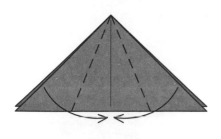  

5. Fold the near flaps inward so that their edges meet along the center line.

6. Fold the corners up and out to the sides so that their upper edges are horizontal.

7. Fold the bottom edges of the two folded flaps up to meet in the middle.

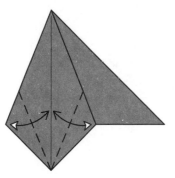 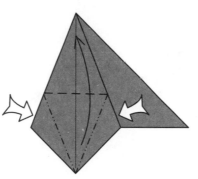 

8. Fold two flaps downward so that their edges meet along the center line.

9. Turn the paper over from side to side.

10. Squash-fold the left flap symmetrically.

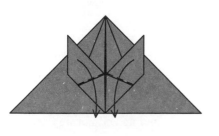 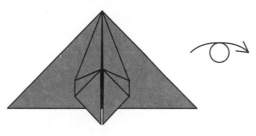 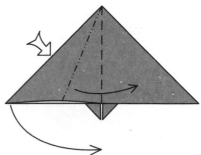

11. Fold the edges in to the center line and unfold.

12. Petal-fold the corner upward.

13. Fold one corner in to the center line.

 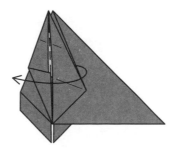 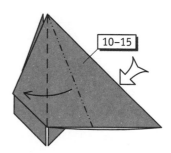

14. Fold and unfold the tip of the near flap to create a pinch mark on the outer edge.

15. Fold one flap to the left.

16. Repeat steps 10–15 in mirror image on the right.

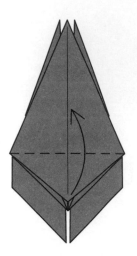

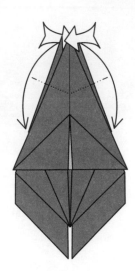

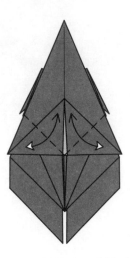

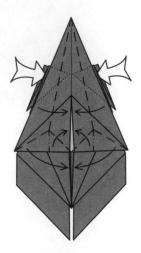

17. Fold one corner upward.

18. Reverse-fold the left point downward, using as a guide the pinch mark you made in step 14. Repeat on the right.

19. Fold and unfold the corners.

20. Fold a rabbit ear from the two lower corners of the near layer and spread the two inner points symmetrically. The inner points will not lie flat.

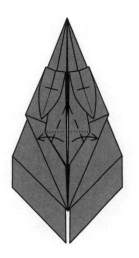

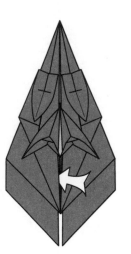

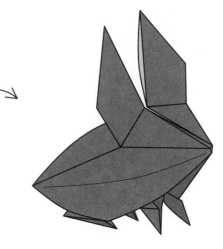

21. Fold the two thick points out to the sides, forming small gussets on the inside.

22. Inflate the body by blowing into the slit shown. Turn the model over.

23. Finished Sitting Bunny.

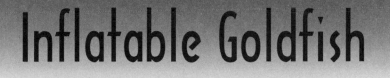

Inflatable Goldfish

Traditional Chinese design, modified by Philip Shen

Use a 6 to 10 inch square.

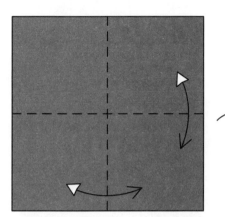

1. Begin with the colored side up. Fold the paper in half vertically and horizontally and unfold. Turn the paper over.

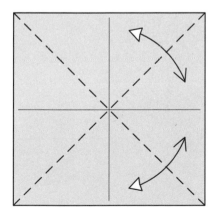

2. Fold the paper in half along both diagonals and unfold.

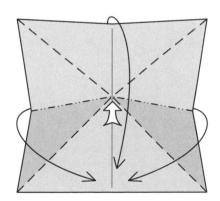

3. Push in the center of the paper and simultaneously bring the middle of three sides to the bottom.

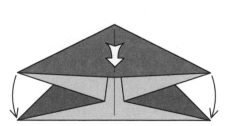

4. Flatten the paper completely, aligning the corners.

 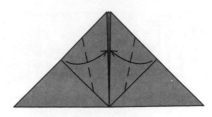 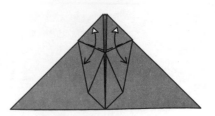

5. Fold the two front corners up to the top of the model.

6. Fold the side corners in to the center line so that they touch each other slightly above the middle of the model.

7. Fold the two top corners down over the folded edges and unfold.

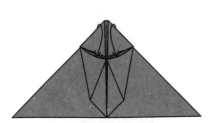 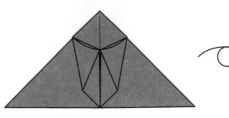 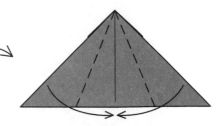

8. Tuck the corners into the pockets.

9. Turn the model over.

10. Fold the outside edges in to meet along the center line.

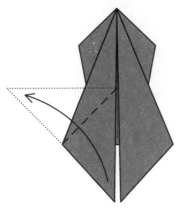 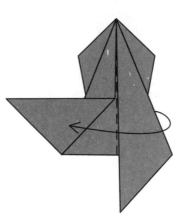

11. Fold the left flap up and out so that its top edge is horizontal.

12. Fold the right flap over to the left.

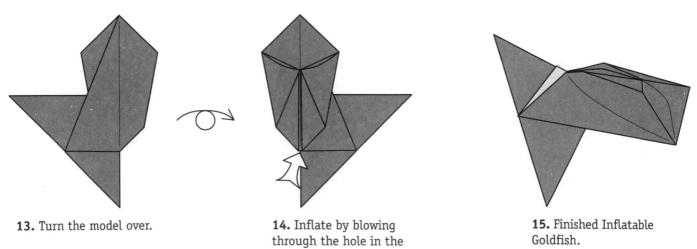

13. Turn the model over.

14. Inflate by blowing through the hole in the bottom.

15. Finished Inflatable Goldfish.

Folding Knife

Designed by Robert J. Lang

With a bit of breaking in, you can get the folding action of this knife as smooth as that of a real pocketknife. Use a 6 inch square to get a pocketknife-sized knife. Foil-backed paper (like wrapping paper) works best.

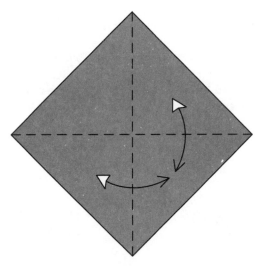

1. Begin with the colored side up. Fold the paper in half and unfold along both diagonals.

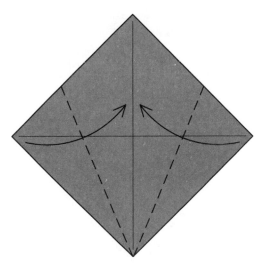

2. Fold the two bottom edges in to the center.

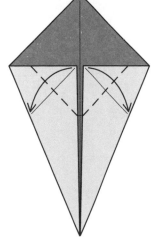

3. Fold each corner down to touch the edge where the crease hits it.

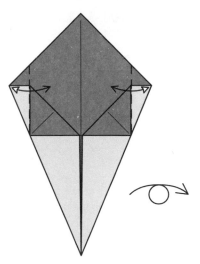

4. Fold each side corner in along the raw edge, crease, and unfold. Then turn the paper over.

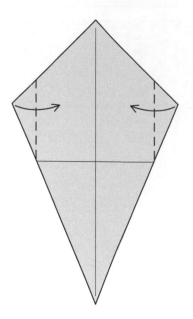 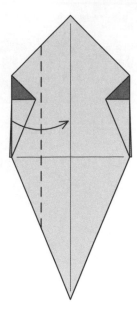 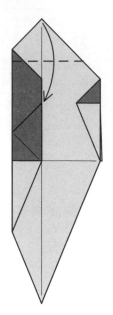 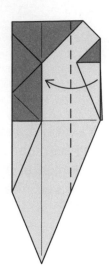

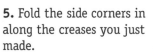

5. Fold the side corners in along the creases you just made.

6. Fold the left edge in to lie along the center line.

7. Fold the top corner down to touch the place where the slanted, folded edge hits the centerline of the model.

8. Fold the right edge in to lie along the centerline of the model.

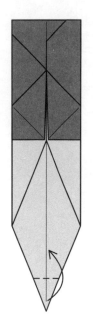 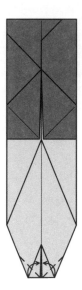 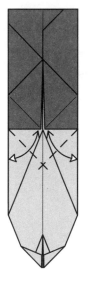 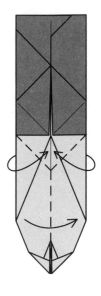

9. Fold a bit of the bottom point upward. The exact amount isn't critical.

10. Fold the two bottom corners in.

11. Fold the left white edge up to lie along the horizontal colored edge; crease from the edge to the center of the model (not all the way) and unfold. Repeat on the right.

12. Fold a rabbit ear from the white flap; leave it standing straight up from the rest of the model.

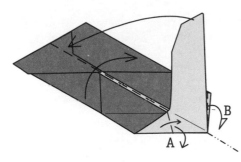 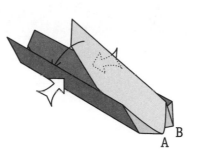 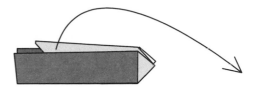

13. Simultaneously fold the body of the knife in half and swivel the blade down to lie between the halves of the body. Make sure you fold edges A and B in half while you do this.

14. In progress. Flatten completely.

15. Unfold to step 13.

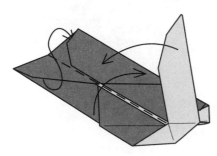 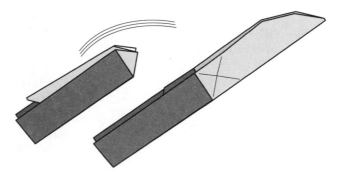

16. Close the model back up as you did in step 13, but this time tuck the flap at the end opposite the blade into the pocket shown.

17. Finished Folding Knife. Watch out for paper cuts!

Barking Wolf

Designed by Robert J. Lang

There are many variations of this basic design.
Use a 6 to 10 inch square.

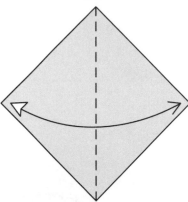

1. Begin with the white side up.
Fold the paper in half vertically
and unfold.

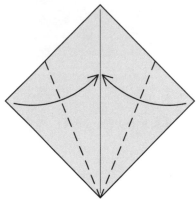

2. Fold the two lower edges in to
meet along the vertical center
line.

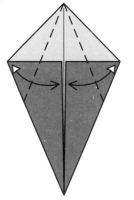

3. Fold the two top edges in to
meet along the center line and
unfold.

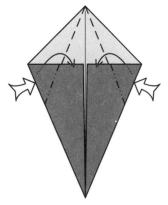

4. Reverse-fold the side corners
inward using the creases you just
made.

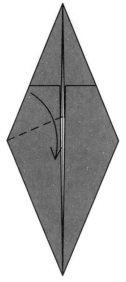

5. Fold the left corner
down as far as possible.

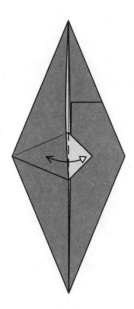

6. Fold the white corner over to the left and unfold.

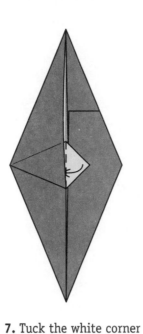

7. Tuck the white corner inside the pocket.

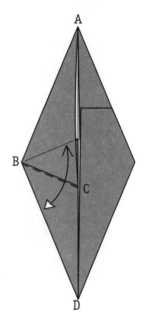

8. Fold edge AB down to edge BC and unfold.

9. Fold edge BD up to the crease you just made and unfold.

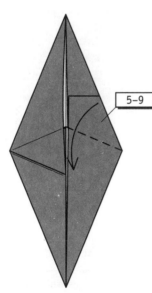

10. Repeat steps 5–9 on the right.

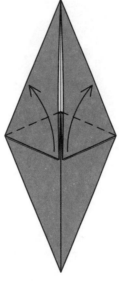

11. Fold the two corners up.

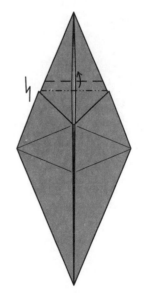

12. Pleat the top flap. Note that the moutain fold lines up with the tops of the two corners.

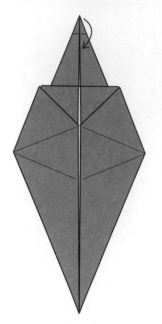

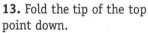

13. Fold the tip of the top point down.

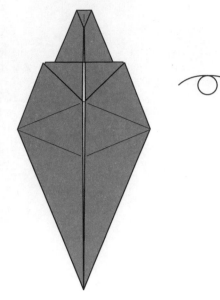

14. Turn the model over.

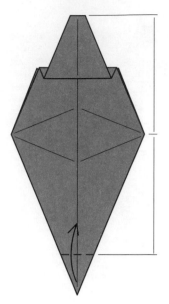

15. Fold the tip of the bottom point up. The top and bottom folded edges should end up being about the same distance from the center of the model, but the exact amount isn't critical.

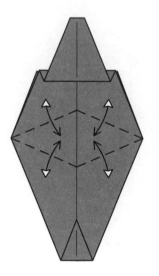

16. Fold and unfold in four places on existing creases.

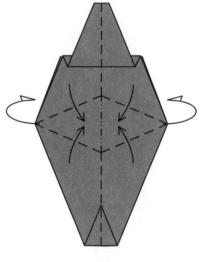

17. Fold the top and bottom points toward each other on the creases you just made and swing the side corners away from you.

18. Finished Barking Wolf. Squeeze the sides of the head. The Wolf will open and close his mouth.

Gobbling Clam

Designed by Robert J. Lang

Use a 6 to 10 inch square.

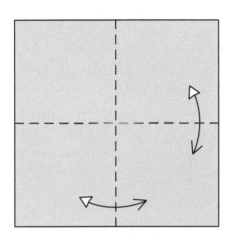

1. Begin with the white side up. Fold the paper in half vertically and horizontally.

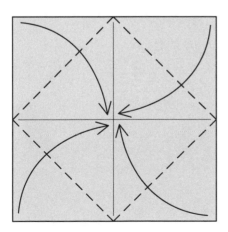

2. Fold the four corners to the center.

3. Turn the paper over.

4. Fold each of the edges in turn to lie along the center line; crease and unfold.

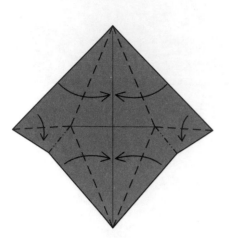 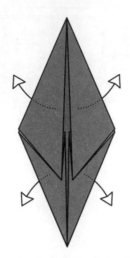 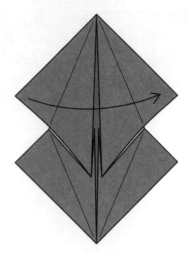

5. Bring all four edges to the center line at once, pinching the side corners together. Flatten the paper with the side corners pointing down.

6. Flip the four flaps in back out to the sides. (They were probably trying to flip out on their own as you did step 5!)

7. Fold the upper left flap over to the right.

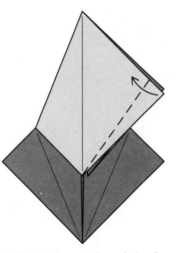 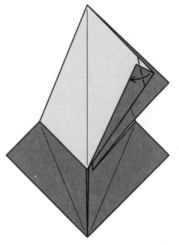

8. Fold the lower edge of the flap upward to make a long, skinny triangle. The exact distance isn't critical.

9. Fold the corner in so that the raw edges line up.

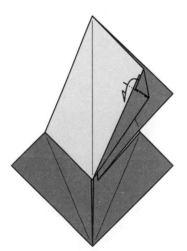 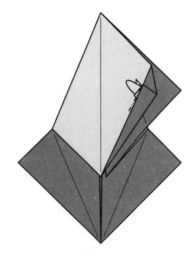 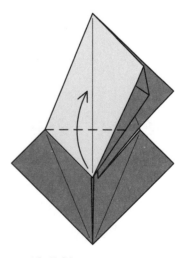

10. Mountain-fold the inner corner downward.

11. Mountain-fold the tiny white corner behind.

12. Fold one corner up.

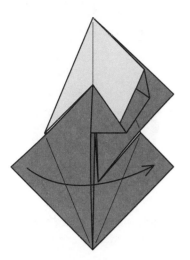

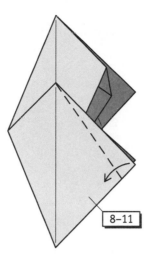

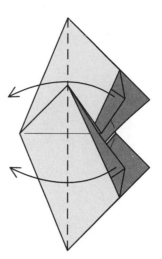

13. Fold the bottom corner to the right.

14. Repeat steps 8–11 on this flap.

15. Fold the top and bottom white flaps together to the left.

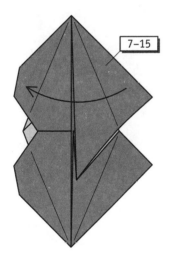

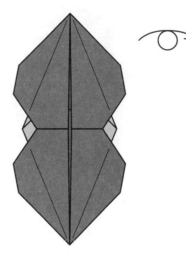

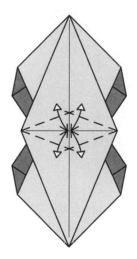

16. Repeat steps 7–15 on the right.

17. Turn the model over.

18. Make creases through all layers that run from each side corner to just above and below the middle of the model, four creases in all. The exact angles aren't critical as long as each pair of creases hits the center line at the same place.

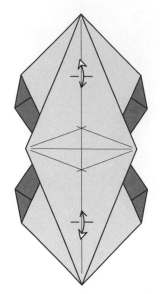

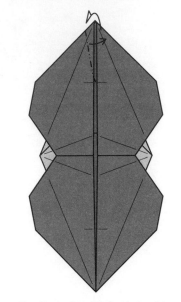

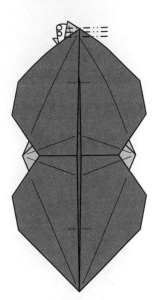

19. Make a small pinch mark on the top and bottom flap. The exact location isn't critical. Turn the paper over.

20. Roll a little bit of the left side near layer over the right side. The far (white) layers will buckle (see step 24). This step is easier if you partially fold the top flap away from you; the middle of the flap will bulge upward.

21. Roll the top of the model over and over and flatten firmly.

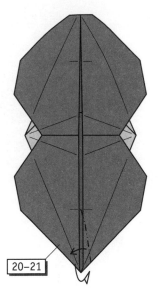

20–21

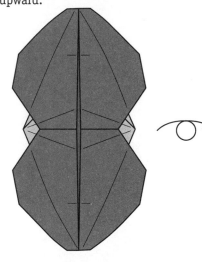

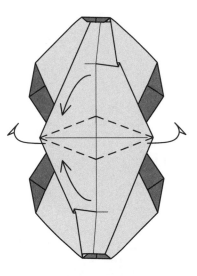

22. Repeat steps 20–21 on the bottom.

23. Turn the paper over.

24. Bring the top and bottom flaps toward each other while curving the side corners slightly away.

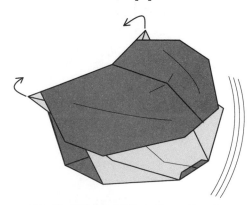

25. Finished Gobbling Clam. Gently squeeze the white corners together and the clam will open and shut its shell.

Talking Frogger

Designed by Nick Robinson

Use a 6 to 10 inch square.

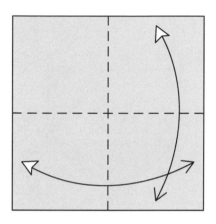

1. Begin with the white side up. Fold the paper in half vertically and horizontally and unfold.

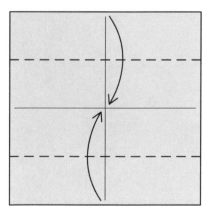

2. Fold the top and bottom edges to the horizontal crease in the center.

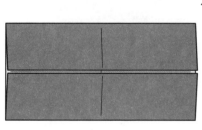

3. Turn the paper over.

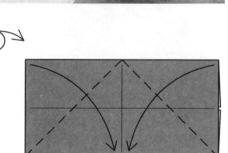

4. Fold the two top corners down to meet at the middle of the bottom edge. Fold all of the layers together as one.

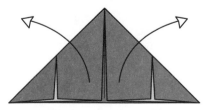

5. Unfold the two corners.

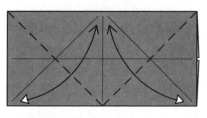

6. Repeat steps 4–5 on the bottom two corners.

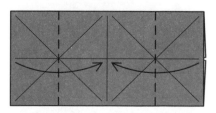

7. Fold the left and right edges in to meet at the vertical center line.

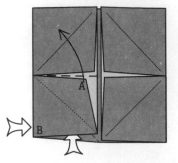

8. Grasp corner A and swing it up toward the upper left corner; at the same time, squash the lower left corner B toward the center of the paper.

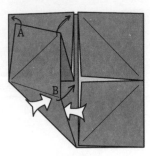

9. In progress. Flatten the paper.

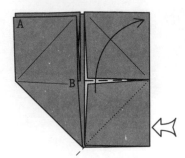

10. Repeat steps 8–9 on the right.

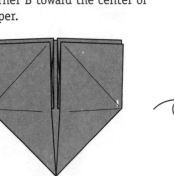

11. Turn the model over from side to side.

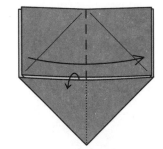

12. Slightly open the pocket at the bottom of the model and fold one flap from left to right, as if you were turning a page of a book.

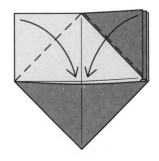

13. Fold one corner down on each side.

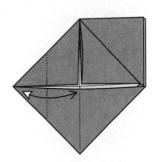

14. Fold the left corner in to the center of the model and unfold, making the crease sharp only in the middle.

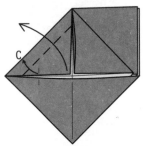

15. Fold the left corner back up beyond the folded edge. The crease should be parallel to the upper left edge, and the crease you just made should touch the edge at point C.

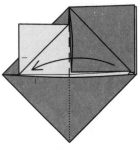

16. Swing the triangular flap back to the left inside the large bottom pocket, covering up the base of the white triangle.

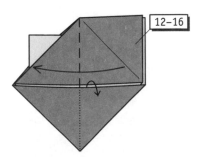

17. Repeat steps 12–16 on the right.

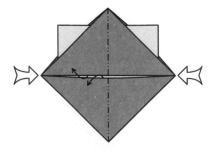

18. Push in the sides and pull out the layers in the center.

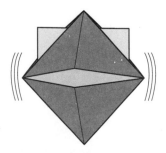

19. Finished Talking Frogger. Squeeze the sides of the head to make him open and close his mouth.

Pecking Woodpecker

Designed by Nick Robinson

By altering the head folds, you can make several different types of woodpecker. Use a 6 to 10 inch square of paper.

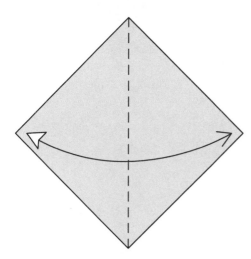

1. Begin with the white side up. Fold the paper in half vertically and unfold.

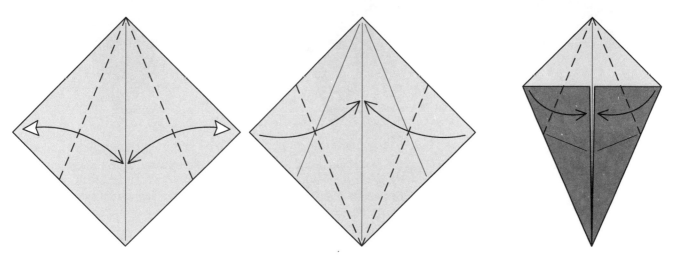

2. Fold the two upper edges in to meet along the vertical center line and unfold.

3. Fold the two lower edges in to meet along the vertical center line.

4. Fold the two top edges in to meet along the center line.

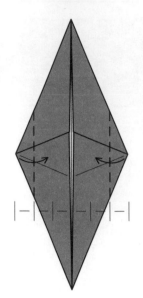

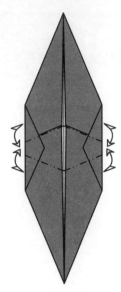

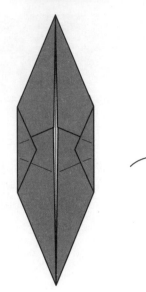

5. Fold the side corners in to about 2/3 of the way to the center (the exact amount isn't critical).

6. Pinch mountain folds at the four places shown. The two upper folds run along folded edges and the two lower ones fall on existing creases on the near layers.

7. Turn the model over.

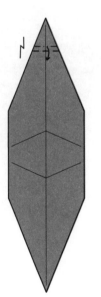

8. Pleat the upper point. The exact amount isn't critical.

9. Fold down the top of the model along a line between the two blunt corners; make the crease sharp only in the middle of the paper and unfold.

10. Fold the top point down to touch the crease you just made; this time, make the crease sharp all the way across and unfold.

11. Fold the model in half.

12. Crimp the head down.

13. Fold the head and neck from side to side, folding through both layers; repeat behind.

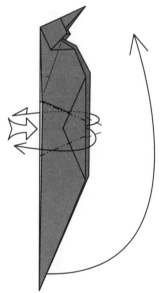

14. Open out the right side; swing the bottom point upward. At the same time, push in the spine of the model in the center.

15. Make sure that the bottom is convex when seen from above.

16. Finished Pecking Woodpecker. Squeeze the base of the model to make the Woodpecker tap the tree.

Catapult

Adapted from traditional designs

Use a 6 to 10 inch square.

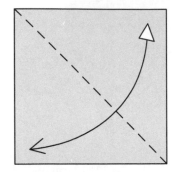

1. Begin with the white side up. Fold the paper in half along the diagonal and unfold.

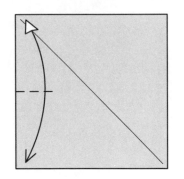

2. Fold the bottom of the paper up to the top, pinch along the left side, and unfold.

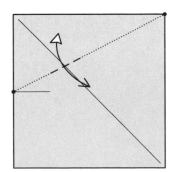

3. Fold the top left corner down along a crease that runs from the pinch to the top right corner. Make the crease sharp only where it crosses the diagonal; then unfold.

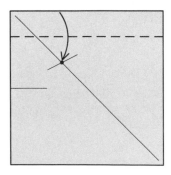

4. Fold the top edge down to touch the intersection of the two creases.

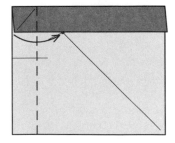

5. Fold the left edge rightward to touch the same point.

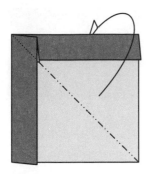 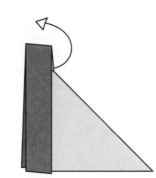 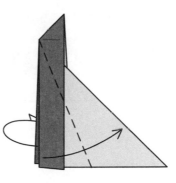 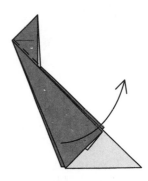

6. Mountain-fold the top right corner behind.

7. Pull the corner out as far as possible.

8. Fold the left edge of the near flap up to lie along the diagonal. Repeat behind.

9. Swing the near flap upward.

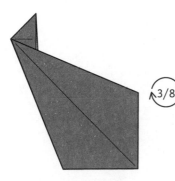 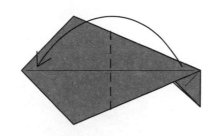 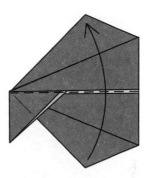

10. Rotate 3/8 turn clockwise.

11. Fold the right point over to the left, but don't make the crease sharp.

12. Fold the bottom half of the model up to match the top. The crease made in step 11 — which now lies at the right — should still not be sharpened.

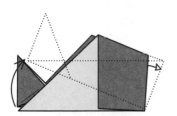 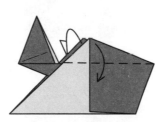 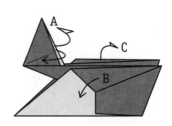

13. Slide the inside point upward so that its upper edge is horizontal. Now flatten the crease at the right firmly so that it stays in place.

14. Fold the near edge down so that the crease lines up with the edge of the flap in the middle. Repeat behind.

15. Open out pocket A slightly; lift corners B and C out away from the rest of the model.

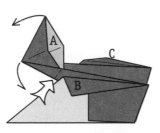 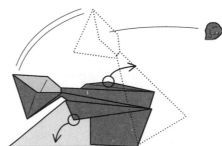

16. Open out pocket A further and bend it downward at its base. The "throat" at the base of the pocket will flatten.

17. Finished Catapult. Put a small wad of paper in the pocket and pull on the two corners sharply; the Catapult will throw its load. With some practice, you can make it throw several feet!

Cootie Catcher

Traditional design

The Cootie Catcher is a favorite playground toy. Depending on how you hold it, two different pockets are exposed in the interior, a property that permits all sorts of tricks!

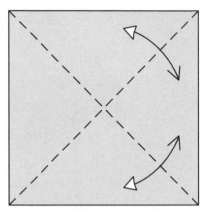

1. Begin with the white side up. Fold the paper in half along each diagonal and unfold.

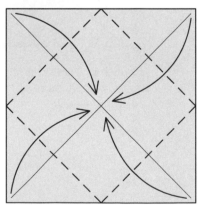

2. Fold the four corners in to the center of the square.

3. Turn the paper over.

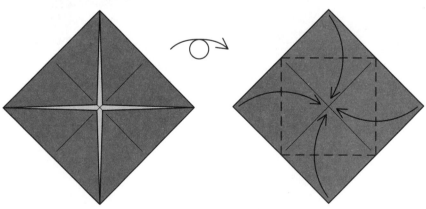

4. Fold the four corners in to the center again.

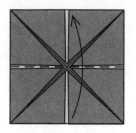

5. Fold the bottom edge up to meet the top edge.

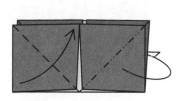

6. Fold the lower left corner up in front; fold the lower right corner behind.

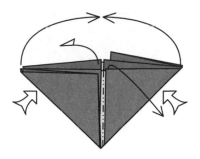

7. Open out the large pocket in the center top and squeeze the sides toward each other.

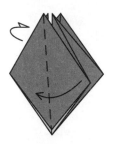

8. Adjust the position of the four flaps so that they all stand straight out from each other.

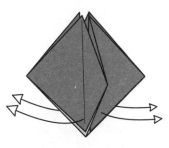

9. Pull out the four colored flaps.

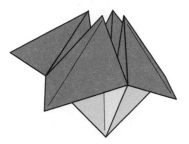

10. Finished Cootie Catcher.

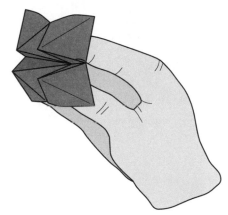

To use the Cootie Catcher, you put your fingers into the pockets underneath the colored flaps, putting one finger in each pocket (your ring finger and pinky can share a pocket). With a little practice, you can open the top of the Catcher in two different ways.

All clean!   Cooties!

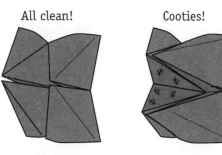

Now, here's where the "Cootie" part comes in: Draw some bugs or other critters on the flaps that are visible one way but covered the other.

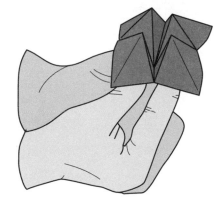

Another way of using the Cootie Catcher is as a "fortune teller." This uses the two-handed grip shown above. You have your subject guess a number, then count it off, alternating between the two positions; the subject then guesses a flap, which is lifted up to reveal a fortune underneath.

Harlequin Cootie Catcher

Designed by Russell Cashdollar

This is a more colorful version of the traditional toy. Use at least a 10 inch square colored on one side.

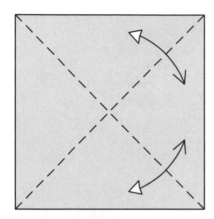

1. Begin with the white side up. Fold the paper in half along each diagonal and unfold.

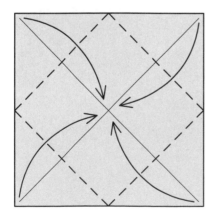

2. Fold the four corners in to the center of the square.

3. Fold the corners back to the outside edges.

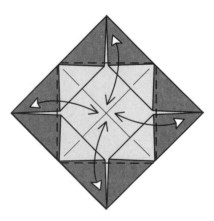

4. Fold the four corners to the center and unfold.

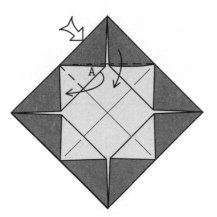

5. Fold the corner down again, but pull point A out and over to the right.

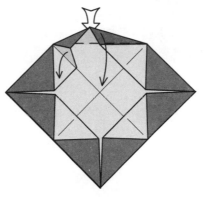

6. In progress.

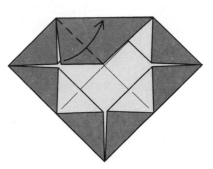

7. Fold the corner back up.

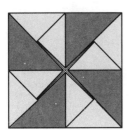

8. Rotate the paper 1/4 turn clockwise.

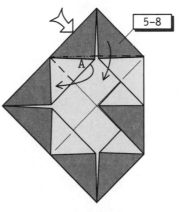

9. Repeat steps 5–8 on the top corner.

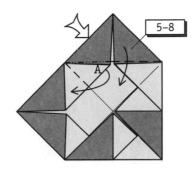

10. Repeat steps 5–8 on the remaining two corners.

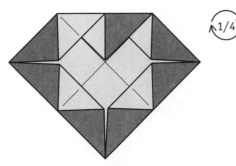

11. Turn the paper over.

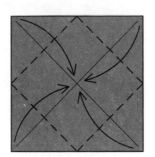

12. Fold the corners in to the center one more time.

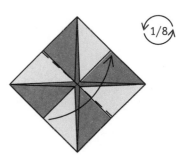

13. Fold the square shape in half, edge to edge, and rotate 1/8 turn counterclockwise.

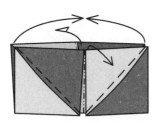

14. Bring the four top corners together and open out the pocket in the center of the top.

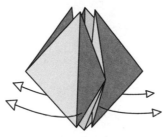

15. Pull out the four flaps.

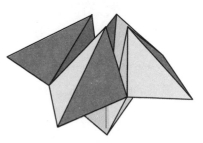

16. Finished Harlequin Cootie Catcher.

Talking Mouse Mask

Designed by Robert J. Lang

Adding ears to the Cootie Catcher makes this puppet. Use a 10 inch square.

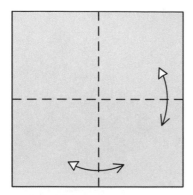

1. Begin with the white side up. Fold and unfold the paper in half vertically and horizontally.

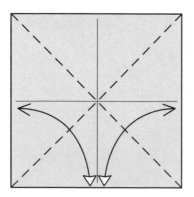

2. Fold and unfold along both diagonals.

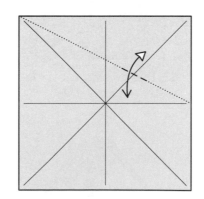

3. Fold the top edge down along a crease that runs from the upper left corner to the midpoint of the right side. Make the crease sharp where it crosses the diagonal and unfold.

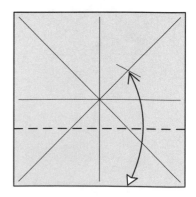

4. Fold the bottom edge up to the intersection of two creases and unfold.

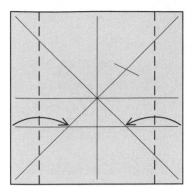

5. Fold the side edges in to the intersection of the diagonal creases and the crease you just made.

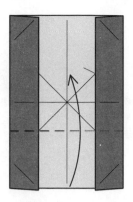

6. Fold the bottom edge up on an existing crease.

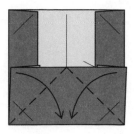

7. Fold two corners down to the bottom edge.

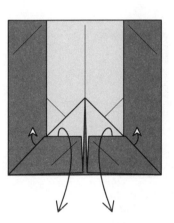

8. Pull the two raw edges downward, releasing some trapped paper.

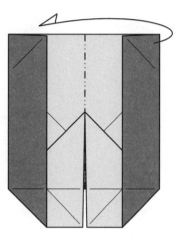

9. Mountain-fold the model in half and rotate 1/4 turn counterclockwise.

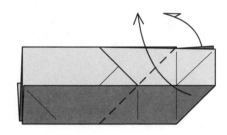

10. Fold the lower right corner upward. Repeat behind.

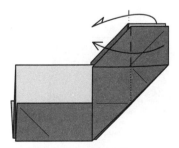

11. Fold the upper right flap to the left; note that the crease runs underneath another layer. Repeat behind.

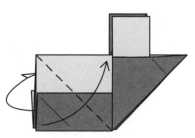

12. Fold the lower left corner up to the middle of the model. Repeat behind.

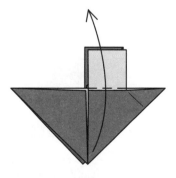

13. Lift up the bottom point as far as possible.

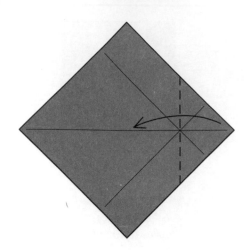 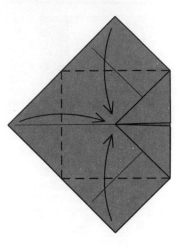 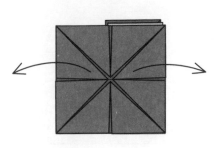

14. Fold the right point as far to the left as possible (the fold runs through the crease intersection shown).

15. Fold the other three points in to meet the right point.

16. Unfold two flaps.

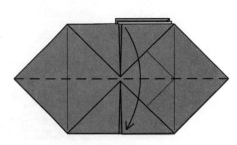 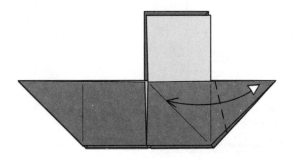

17. Fold the top flap down.

18. Fold the right point over to touch the diagonal crease (the exact location isn't important); crease firmly and unfold.

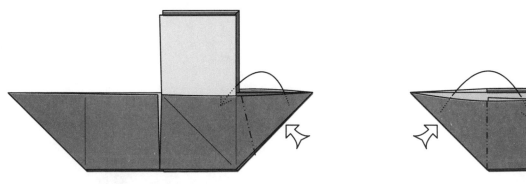 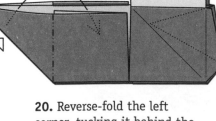

19. Reverse-fold the right corner, tucking it behind the white flap.

20. Reverse-fold the left corner, tucking it behind the near layer of paper.

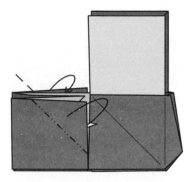

21. Mountain-fold about 2/3 of the the corner underneath. Repeat behind.

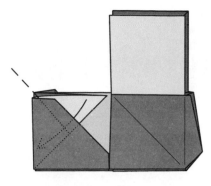

22. Tuck the white triangle as far down into the pocket as it will go.

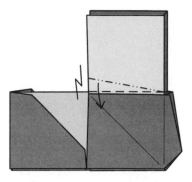

23. Make a zig-zag pleat at the base of the white flap. Repeat behind.

24. Mountain-fold the top corners of the white flap to round them. Then round the lower left corner with a tiny reverse fold. Repeat behind.

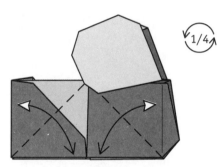

25. Fold and unfold. Rotate the model 1/4 turn counterclockwise.

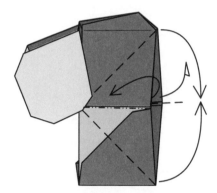

26. Open out the pocket on the right, spreading its edges. At the same time, bring the upper and lower right corners together. The model becomes three-dimensional.

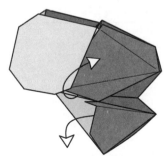

27. Pull out four flaps, two in front and to behind.

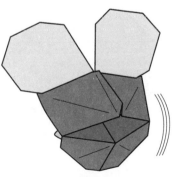

28. Finished Talking Mouse Mask. Put your fingers in the pockets behind the face to make the mouth open and close.

Talking Dragon

Traditional design

Use a 6 to 10 inch square.

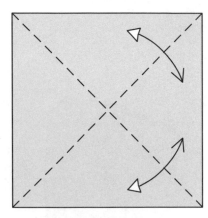

1. Begin with the white side up. Fold the paper in half along each diagonal and unfold.

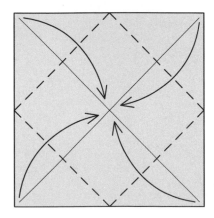

2. Fold the four corners in to the center of the square.

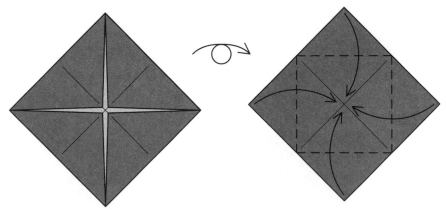

3. Turn the paper over.

4. Fold the four corners in to the center again.

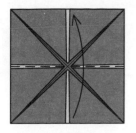

5. Fold the bottom edge up to meet the top edge.

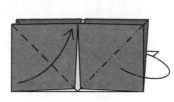

6. Fold the lower left corner up in front; fold the lower right corner behind.

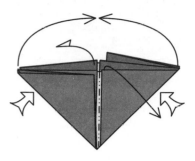

7. Open out the large pocket in the center top and squeeze the sides toward each other.

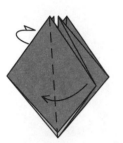

8. Adjust the position of the four flaps so that they all stand straight out from each other.

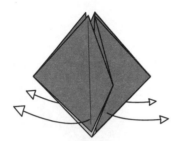

9. Pull out the four colored flaps.

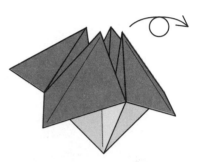

10. This is the traditional Cootie Catcher. Turn the model over.

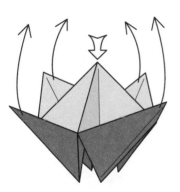

11. Push down on the middle and turn the middle of the model inside-out.

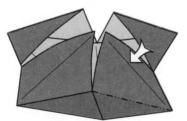

12. Push one of the four flaps down inside the model.

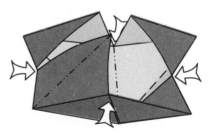

13. Squeeze the centers of all four sides together.

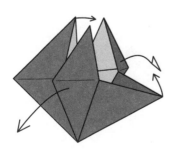

14. Pull two opposite corners apart.

15. Finished Talking Dragon. Hold the wings and move them in and out to make the Dragon talk.

Kicking Frog

Designed by Robert J. Lang

This frog is unusual among the many origami frogs in that he actually kicks his legs. Use a 10 inch square.

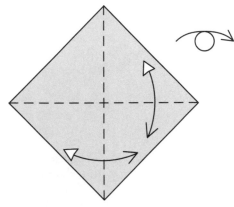

1. Begin with the white side up. Fold the paper in half along the diagonals and unfold. Turn the paper over.

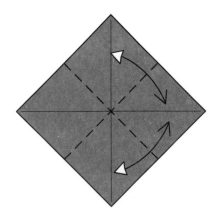

2. Fold and unfold by bringing one edge to the opposite edge. Do this in both directions.

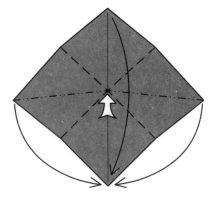

3. Push in the center and bring all four corners together at the bottom.

4. Flatten the paper.

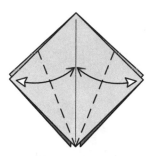 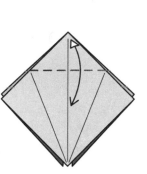 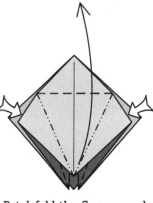 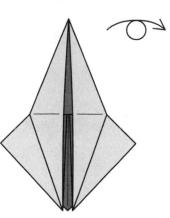

5. Fold the sides of the front flaps in to the center line and unfold.

6. Fold the top point down and unfold.

7. Petal-fold the flap upward.

8. Turn the model over.

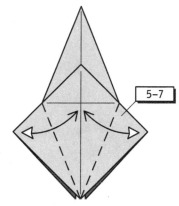 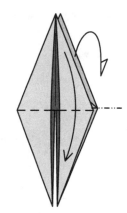 

5–7

9. Repeat steps 5–7 on this side.

10. Fold one flap down in front and behind.

11. Fold one flap to the right.

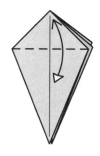 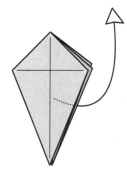 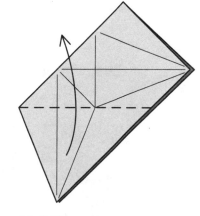 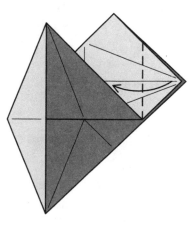

12. Fold and unfold.

13. Pull the middle flap out completely.

14. Fold one flap up on an existing crease.

15. Fold one corner over to line up with an edge.

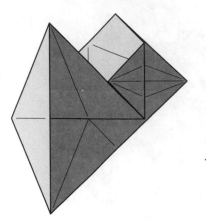

16. Turn the paper over.

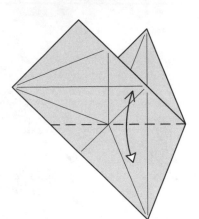

17. Fold and unfold.

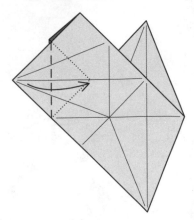

18. Fold the corner over to match the corner underneath.

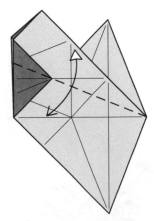

19. Fold and unfold to the horizontal crease through a single flap.

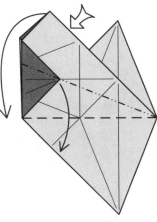

20. Squash-fold the flap.

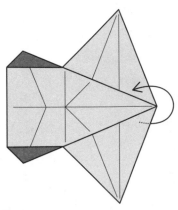

21. Wrap one layer from back to front.

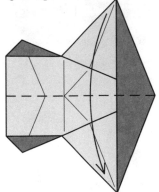

22. Fold the model in half.

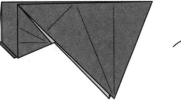

23. Turn the model over.

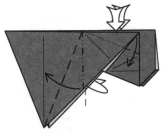

24. Swivel-fold. Repeat behind.

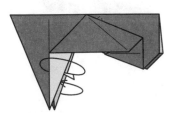

25. Fold the flaps inside.

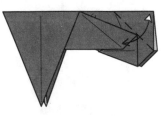

26. Fold and unfold.

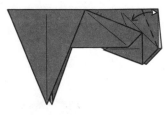

27. Fold and unfold.

Origami in Action 80

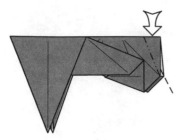

28. Reverse-fold the corner.

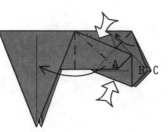

29. Squash-fold the edge over to the left. Watch the positions of corners A, B, and C.

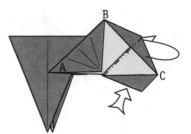

30. Repeat step 29 behind.

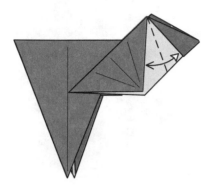

31. Fold raw edge to raw edge and unfold.

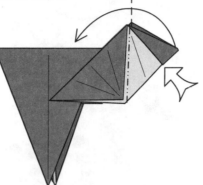

32. Reverse-fold the corner between the two near layers.

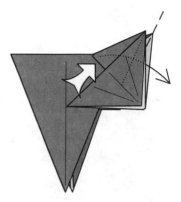

33. Reverse-fold the corner back to the left using the crease you made in step 31.

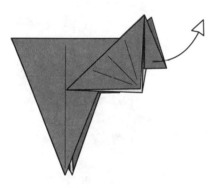

34. Unfold to step 31 again.

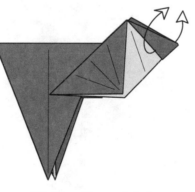

35. Open the model at the right and unwrap one layer as shown.

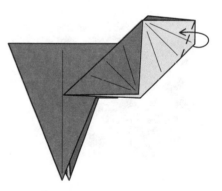

36. Fold one corner over.

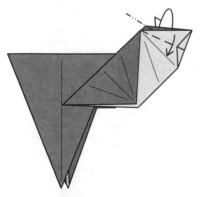

37. Outside reverse-fold on existing creases.

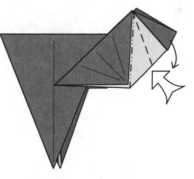

38. Restore the reverse folds from steps 32–33.

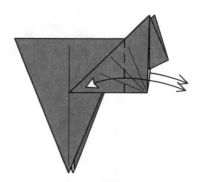

39. Fold the loose flap from left to right and unfold. Repeat behind.

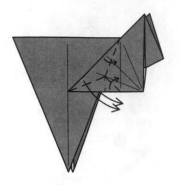

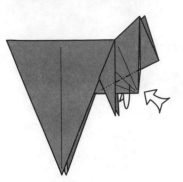

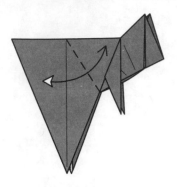

40. Fold a rabbit ear. Repeat behind.

41. Reverse-fold the edge inside.

42. Fold and unfold through all layers.

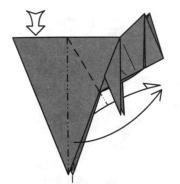

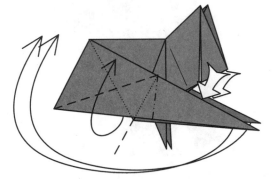

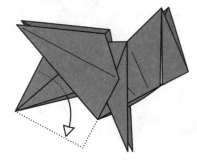

43. Crimp the two lower points over to the right on existing creases.

44. Squash-fold the point upward and to the left. Repeat behind.

45. Open out the rear and pull out a single layer of paper.

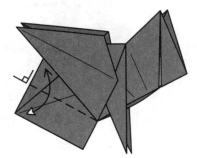

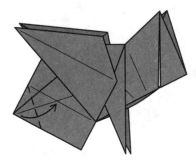

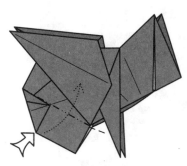

46. Fold and unfold.

47. Fold the thick corner up to lie along the crease line.

48. Carefully closed-sink the corner up inside the model.

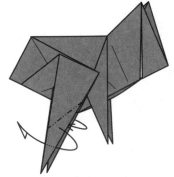

49. Pinch the left flaps (the legs) in half and swing them down.

50. Mountain-fold the near leg underneath. Repeat behind.

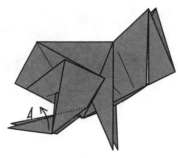
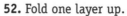

51. Crease lightly. Repeat behind.

52. Fold one layer up.

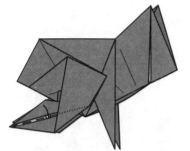

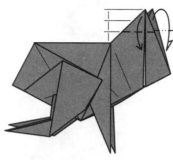

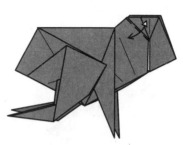

53. Tuck the colored flap into the white pocket. Repeat behind.

54. Fold down 2/3 of the top point. Repeat behind.

55. Fold and unfold along the edge through the near layers. Repeat behind.

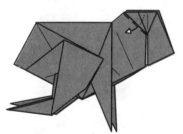

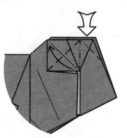

56. Pull out a single layer of paper; flatten.

57. Detail of head. Squash-fold the upper corner.

58. Loosen the colored flap and wrap it to the inside. Repeat steps 56–58 behind.

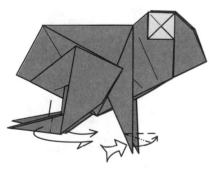

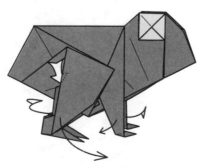

59. Mountain-fold the hind legs underneath. Squash-fold the tips of the front legs out flat.

60. Spread the hind legs out to the sides so the feet lie flat. Spread the front legs as well.

61. Finished Kicking Frog. Pull on the head and rear; the frog will kick his legs behind him.

Wagging-Tail Doggie

Designed by Robert J. Lang

Use a 6 to 10 inch square of paper.

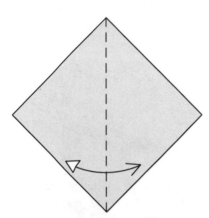

1. Begin with the white side up. Fold the paper in half vertically and unfold.

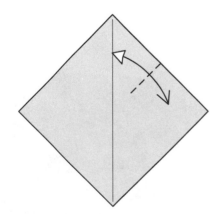

2. Fold the top corner down to the right corner and crease near the edge. Unfold.

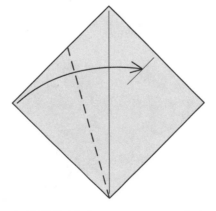

3. Fold the left corner over so that it lies on the crease you just made.

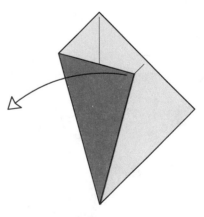

4. Unfold.

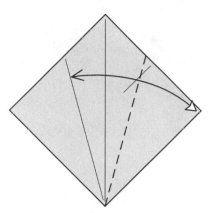

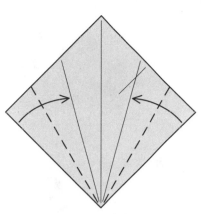

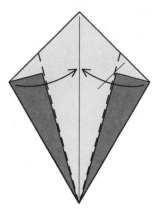

5. Fold the right edge over to lie along the crease you just made and unfold.

6. Fold both the lower right and lower left edges in to lie along the existing creases.

7. Fold the left and right edges in to meet at the center line.

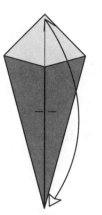

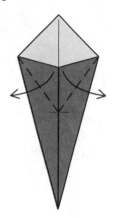

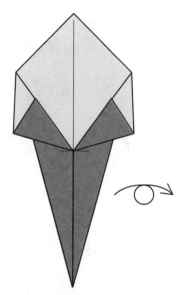

8. Fold the bottom point up to the top and make a small pinch through all layers in the center. Unfold.

9. Fold the corners out to the side. Note that the creases hit the middle edge where you made the pinch mark.

10. Turn the paper over.

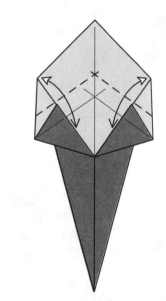

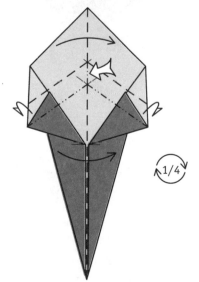

11. Fold the left edge down to line up with the short nearly-horizontal edge and unfold. Repeat on the right and turn the model over again.

12. Fold the left corner down to touch the folded edge; note where the valley fold hits the colored edge. Repeat on the right.

13. Fold the model in half vertically, incorporating pleats from the creases you made in steps 11–12. Rotate the model 1/4 turn clockwise.

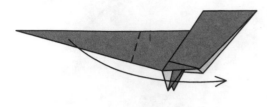  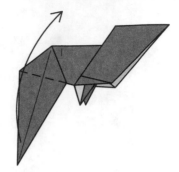

14. Fold the tail over to the right so that its bottom edge lines up with the edge underneath.

15. Squash-fold the flap symmetrically.

16. Valley-fold the point upward, but don't make the crease sharp.

  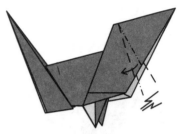

17. Mountain-fold the point behind.

18. Slide the tail to the left so that its edge lines up with the hidden edge. Press flat and make all creases sharp.

19. Crimp the edges of the head.

20. Crimp the head again.

21. Outside reverse-fold the tip of the nose.

22. Pull the tail down so it is nearly flat.

23. Finished Wagging-Tail Doggie. Hold the Doggie and squeeze the rear legs and it will wag its tail. Or, you can hold the tail and squeeze the sides and the Doggie will jump up and down!

Gliding Butterfly

Designed by Makoto Yamaguchi

This butterfly doesn't flap, but it glides as well as any airplane. Use a 6 to 10 inch square.

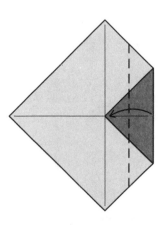

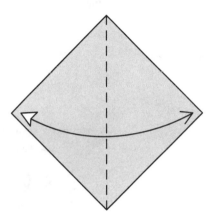

1. Begin with the white side up. Fold the paper in half from side to side and unfold.

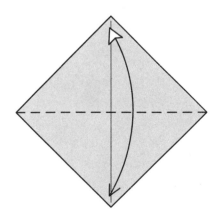

2. Fold the paper in half from top to bottom and unfold.

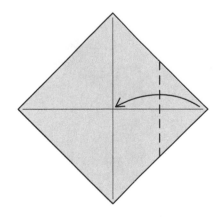

3. Fold the right corner in to the center of the paper.

4. Fold the right edge in to lie along the vertical crease.

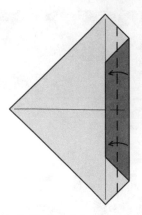

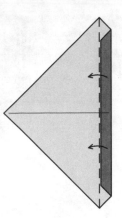

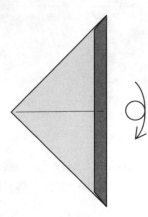

5. Fold the right edge in again to lie along the vertical crease.

6. Fold the right edge over to the left using the existing crease.

7. Turn the paper over from top to bottom.

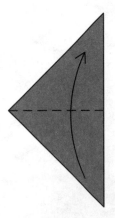

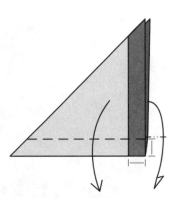

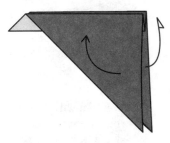

8. Fold the bottom point up to the top point. Flatten firmly, especially at the thick edge along the right side.

9. Fold one flap down in front and one down behind. Note that the distance from the bottom edge to the fold is about the same as the width of the vertical colored layer.

10. Fold both wings back up so they stand straight out from the body.

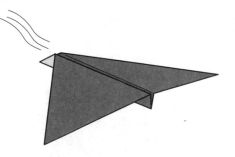

11. Finished Gliding Butterfly. Throw the butterfly lightly to make it glide.

Hovercraft

Designed by Makoto Yamaguchi

Use a 6 to 10 inch square.

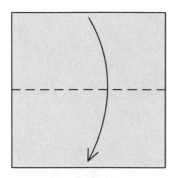

1. Begin with the white side up. Fold the top half of the paper down.

2. Fold one corner up in front; repeat behind.

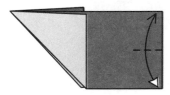

3. Fold one layer in front up to the top edge; make a small pinch near the right side, then unfold.

4. Fold the upper right corner down and unfold. The crease line connects the middle of the top edge and the middle of the right edge.

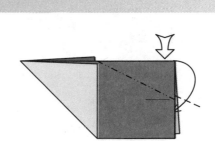

5. Reverse-fold the corner down inside the model on the existing creases.

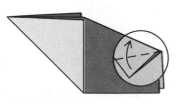

6. Fold the white corner inside the model upward to lock the right side.

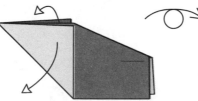

7. Turn the model over and fold down the white flaps. Open out the bottom.

8. Finished Hovercraft. Blow gently into the back of the hovercraft, and it will glide along a flat surface.

Boardsailor

Designed by Nick Robinson

This model will sail on water or on a flat surface such as a desk or tabletop. For water use, foil-backed paper (or even aluminum foil) will float without getting waterlogged. Use a 6 to 10 inch square.

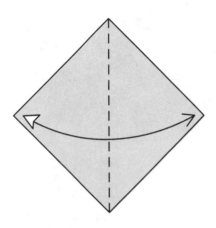

1. Begin with the white side up. Fold the paper in half vertically and unfold.

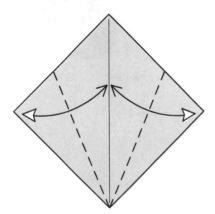

2. Fold the two lower edges in to meet along the vertical center line and unfold.

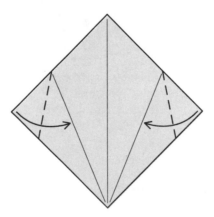

3. Fold the two side corners in so that their upper edges lie along the creases you just made.

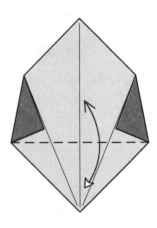

4. Fold the bottom corner up; crease and unfold.

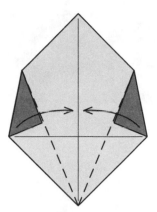

5. Fold the sides in using the existing creases.

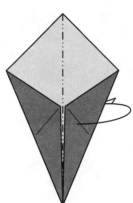

6. Mountain-fold the model in half.

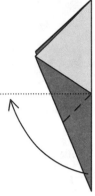

7. Valley-fold the point up on an existing crease.

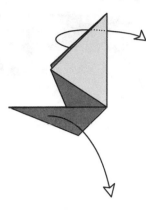

8. Unfold to step 6.

9. Valley-fold the model in half.

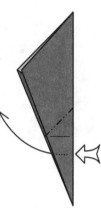

10. Reverse-fold the point up to the left using the existing creases.

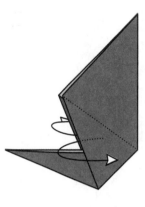

11. Pull a corner out from inside of the model and wrap it around to the right in front. Repeat behind.

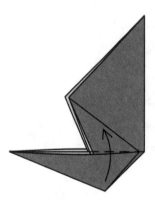

12. Fold one layer up in front.

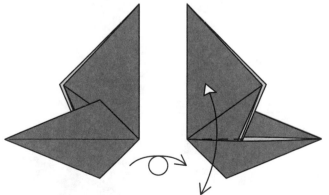

13. Turn the model over.

14. Fold the top flap down and back up.

15. Open out the right side of the top flap and partially squash-fold the left side so that the sail stands straight up from the board.

16. Finished Boardsailor. If you blow gently, the board-sailor will sail on calm water.

Rocking Sailboat

Designed by Gay Merrill Gross

While you can fold this model from almost any size paper, the smaller the paper is, the better it will rock. A 6 to 10 inch square is a good compromise between size and ease of folding.

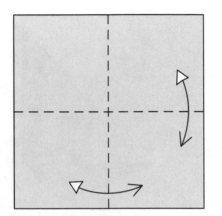

1. This model is folded from an unusual shape, a 60° rhombus. Steps 1–8 show how to cut one from a square. Begin with the white side up. Fold the paper in half vertically and horizontally and unfold.

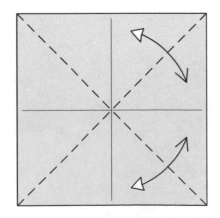

2. Fold the paper in half along both diagonals and unfold.

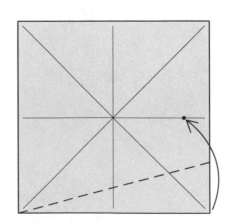

3. Fold the bottom right corner up to touch the horizontal crease.

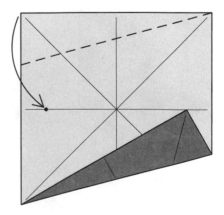

4. Repeat on the upper left corner.

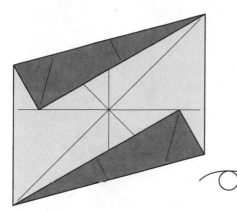

5. Turn the paper over.

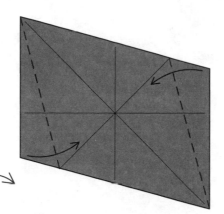

6. Fold the bottom left corner inward. Note that the crease hits the bottom edge at the same place that an existing crease hits it. Do the same thing with the upper right corner.

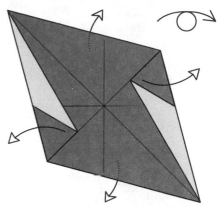

7. Unfold the paper completely and turn it over so the white side is up.

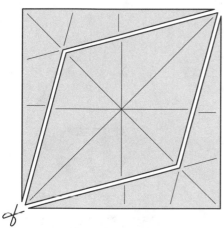

8. Cut off the edges along the crease lines.

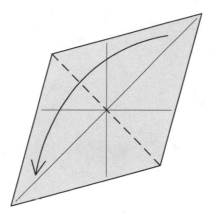

9. Fold the rhombus in half and rotate 1/8 turn counterclockwise.

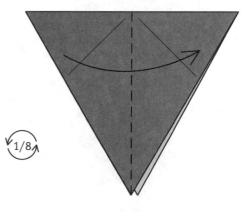

10. Fold the paper in half from left to right.

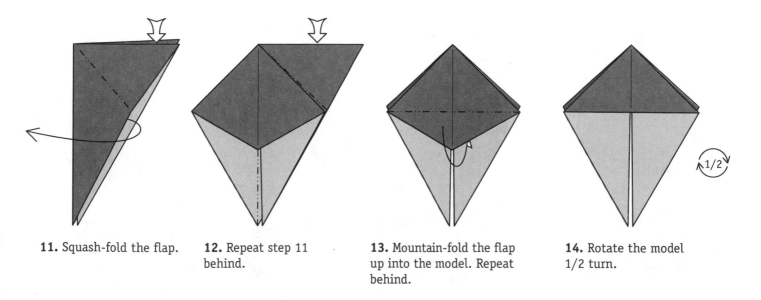

11. Squash-fold the flap.

12. Repeat step 11 behind.

13. Mountain-fold the flap up into the model. Repeat behind.

14. Rotate the model 1/2 turn.

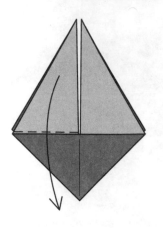

15. Fold one point down along the colored edge.

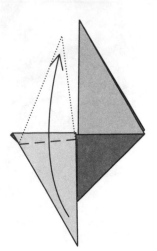

16. Fold the point back upward, angled slightly to the left.

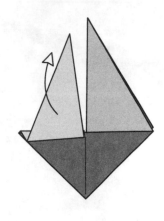

17. Unfold to step 15.

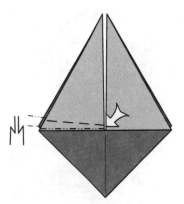

18. Crimp the point on the existing creases.

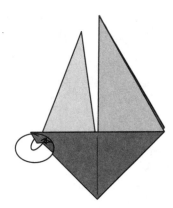

19. Valley-fold both of the partially hidden corners together up inside the model as far as possible.

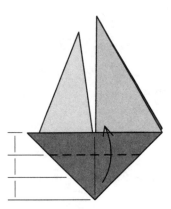

20. Fold 2/3 of the point up and crease firmly.

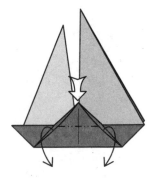

21. Spread the edges on each side of the point and squash the middle of the point. Don't flatten it completely.

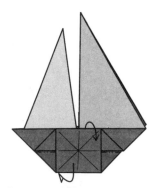

22. Pivot the base of the model so it is perpendicular to the rest of the model.

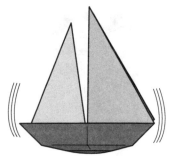

23. Finished Rocking Sailboat, which rocks on its base. Temporarily unlock the folded corners (step 19) and slip a penny inside the square base pocket to stabilize it.

Flying Fighter

Designed by Robert J. Lang

You can modify this model to make many different types of fighter aircraft! It's rather tricky to balance properly for flying. Use a 12 inch square.

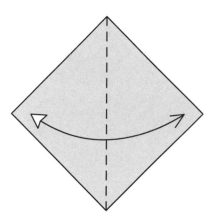

1. Begin with the white side up. Fold and unfold along one diagonal.

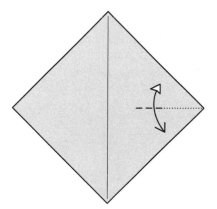

2. Fold one corner in half, pinching sharply only where shown in the drawing.

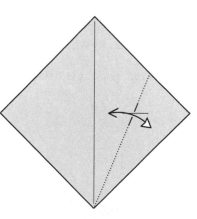

3. Fold along the angle bisector, but only make the crease sharp where it crosses the crease you made in step 2.

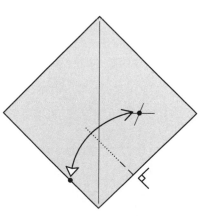

4. Fold the lower left edge up to touch the intersection of the two creases, making sure the lower right raw edges are aligned; make a pinch mark along the lower right edge and unfold.

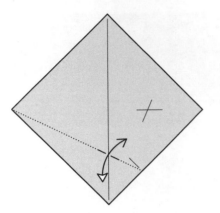

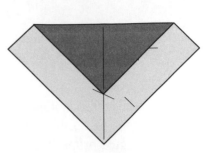

5. Make a crease that connects the mark you just made with the left corner, making the crease sharp only where it crosses the diagonal.

6. Fold the top corner down to touch the intersection of the two creases.

7. Turn the paper over.

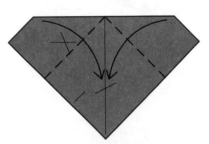

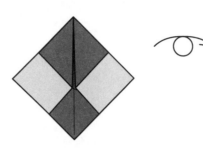

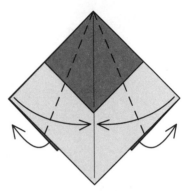

8. Fold the two top corners down so that their edges meet in the middle.

9. Turn the model over.

10. Fold the upper edges in to meet in the center, allowing the flaps behind to swing outward.

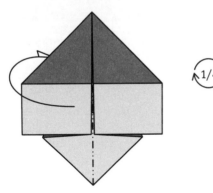

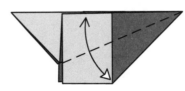

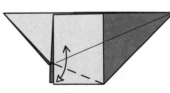

11. Mountain-fold the model in half and rotate 1/4 turn clockwise.

12. Fold the lower right edge of the near flap up to the top and unfold. Repeat behind.

13. Fold the lower left corner upward along a crease that connects the lower right corner with the end of the crease you just made and unfold. Repeat behind.

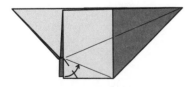

14. Fold the lower left corner of the near layer upward so that its edge lines up with the crease you just made. Repeat behind.

15. Fold the lower corner of the near layer upward along the crease you made in step 13. Repeat behind.

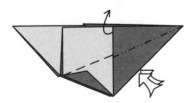

16. Squash-fold the near flap upward. Repeat behind.

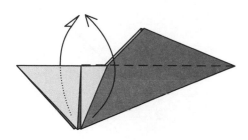

17. Fold one layer up in front and behind.

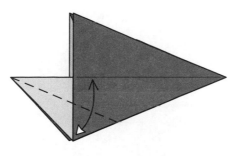

18. Fold the lower left edge up to the horizontal crease and unfold. Repeat behind.

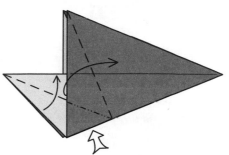

19. Swivel the vertical edge over to the right, squashing the bottom edge. Repeat behind.

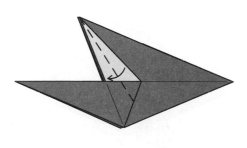

20. Fold the raw edge over to line up with the folded edge. Repeat behind.

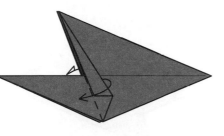

21. Fold the narrow edge over the left. Repeat behind.

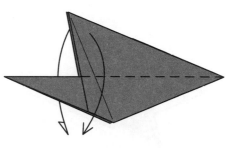

22. Fold one flap down on each side.

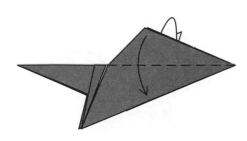

23. Fold one more flap down. Repeat behind.

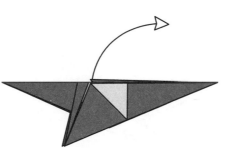

24. Pull the central point all the way out.

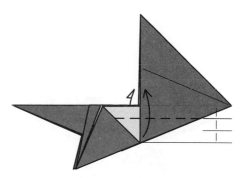

25. Fold 2/3 of the lower near flap upward. Repeat behind.

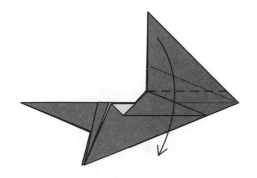

26. Fold the top point down. Note that the crease hits the corner of the flap you just folded up.

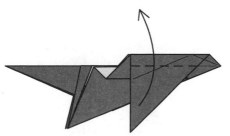

27. Fold the flap back upward. Note that the crease lines up with an existing horizontal crease and edge.

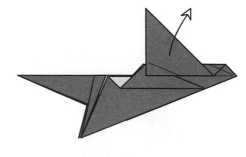

28. Unfold to step 25.

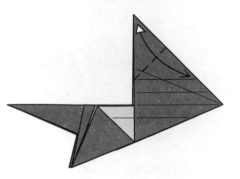

29. Fold the top point down and unfold.

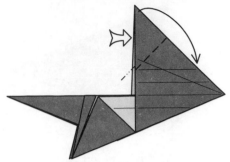

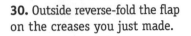

30. Outside reverse-fold the flap on the creases you just made.

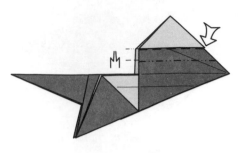

31. Reverse-fold in and out on the existing creases.

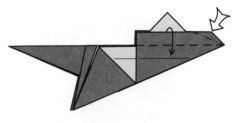

32. Fold one edge downward and squash the corner symmetrically.

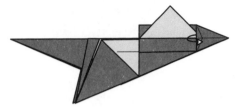

33. Grasp the edge of the white flap where it goes into the pocket; pull it out of the pocket and bring the tip to the front. Flatten.

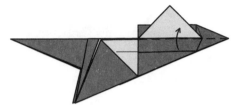

34. Fold the edge back up.

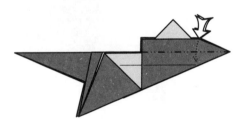

35. Closed-sink two corners down into the model. The two corners go on either side of the middle white edge (as viewed from the top).

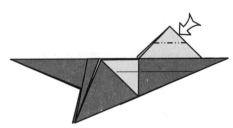

36. Reverse-fold the top of the white flap.

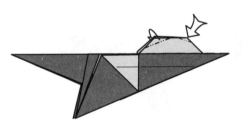

37. Sink the right corner. Mountain-fold the two left corners into the model.

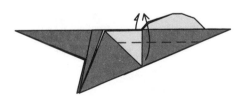

38. Fold one flap up in front and behind on the existing creases.

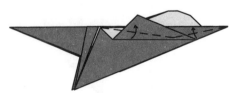

39. Fold the two corners of the horizontal edge upward, forming a tiny rabbit ear where the two creases connect. Repeat behind.

40. Swing the thick edge upward and simultaneously swing the two top flaps down and tuck them inside the model. Repeat behind.

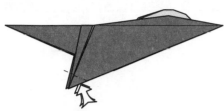

41. Reverse-fold the tips of the wings.

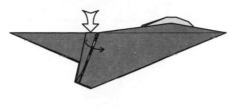
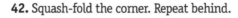

42. Squash-fold the corner. Repeat behind.

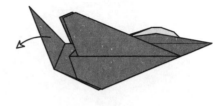

43. Tuck the edge into the pocket underneath. Repeat behind.

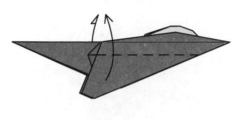

44. Fold the wings up.

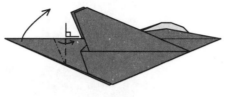

45. Pleat the tail upward.

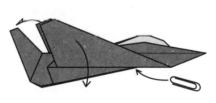

46. Unfold.

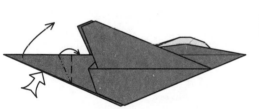

47. Crimp the tail upward, using the creases you just made.

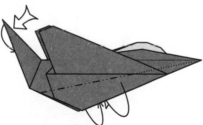

48. Reverse-fold the tip of the tail. Mountain-fold the bottom edges inside.

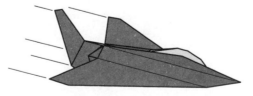

49. Fold the wings outward. For best flying performance, clip a paper clip around the middle layers along the bottom.

50. Finished Flying Fighter. Adjust the position of the paper clip along the body to get the best flight performance.

Clapping Seal

Designed by Robert J. Lang

This model, like the Manatee that follows, makes use of yet another variation of the versatile action mechanism from Randlett's Flapping Bird. Use a 6 to 10 inch square.

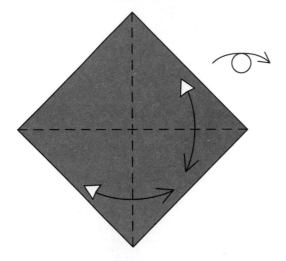

1. Begin with the colored side up. Fold the paper in half along the diagonals and unfold. Turn the paper over.

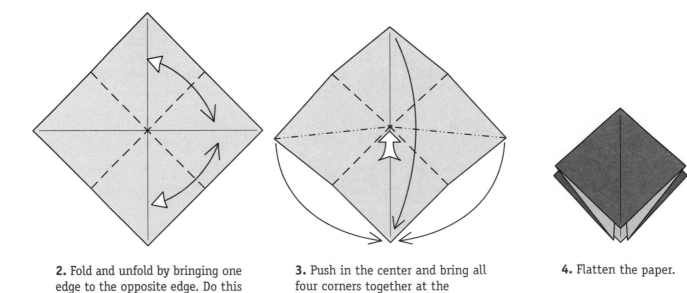

2. Fold and unfold by bringing one edge to the opposite edge. Do this in both directions.

3. Push in the center and bring all four corners together at the bottom.

4. Flatten the paper.

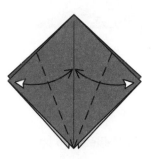

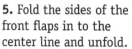

5. Fold the sides of the front flaps in to the center line and unfold.

6. Fold the top point down and unfold.

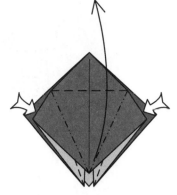

7. Petal-fold the flap upward. To do this, lift up one corner while holding down the top of the model just above the horizontal crease and let the sides swing in.

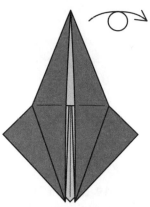

8. Turn the model over.

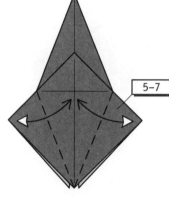

9. Repeat steps 5–7 on this side.

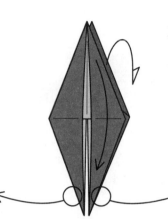

10. Pull the two bottom flaps as far out to the sides as possible and let the two top flaps swing down in front and behind. The center "hump" should pop down, forming a long valley or groove along the top of the model.

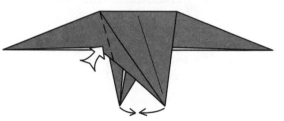

11. Flatten the model completely.

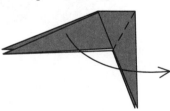

12. Fold the model in half.

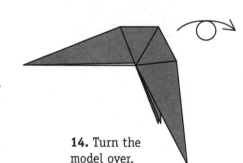

13. Fold one flap over to the right. Note that the crease runs from notch to corner.

14. Turn the model over.

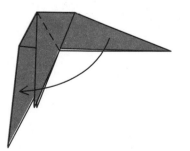

15. Fold the right flap down to match up with the left side.

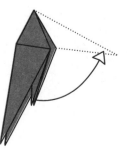

16. Pull one flap out completely.

17. Fold one flap up to the right.

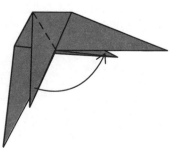

18. Fold one more flap up to the right.

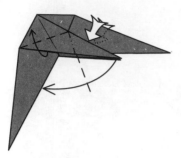

19. Squash-fold the corner down. Repeat behind.

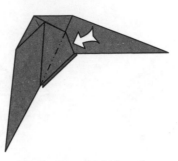

20. Reverse-fold the edge. Repeat behind.

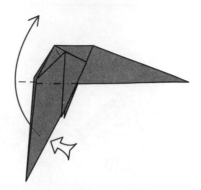

21. Reverse-fold the left flap upward as far as possible.

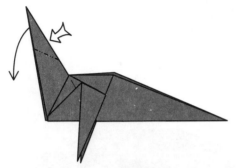

22. Reverse-fold the left flap downward to make a head.

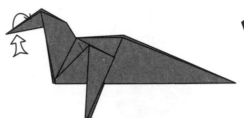

23. Reverse-fold the left point to make a blunt nose.

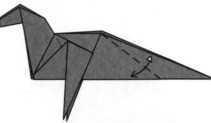

24. Fold and unfold through both layers. The exact angle isn't critical.

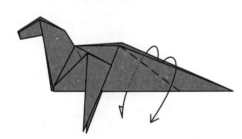

25. Outside reverse-fold using the existing creases.

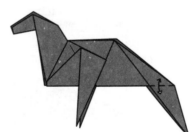

26. Fold and unfold.

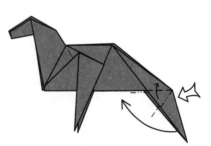

27. Squash-fold the tail to the left and open it out flat.

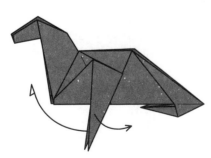

28. Pull out the flippers so that they stand straight out from the body.

29. Finished Clapping Seal. Hold the chest and back and pull. The Seal will clap his flippers together.

Swimming Manatee

Designed by Robert J. Lang

Use a 6 to 10 inch square.

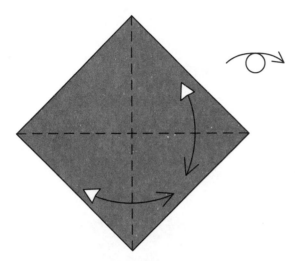

1. Begin with the colored side up. Fold the paper in half along the diagonals and unfold. Turn the paper over.

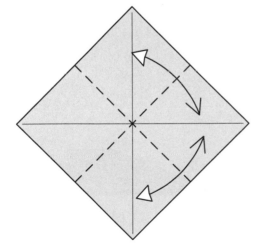

2. Fold and unfold by bringing one edge to the opposite edge. Do this in both directions.

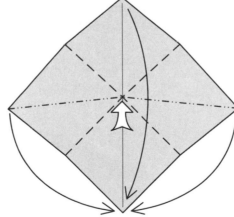

3. Push in the center and bring all four corners together at the bottom.

4. Flatten the paper.

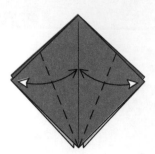 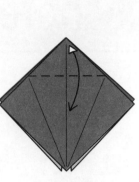 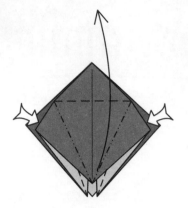 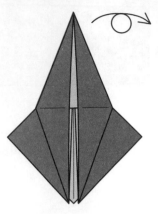

5. Fold the sides of the front flaps in to the center line and unfold.

6. Fold the top point down and unfold.

7. Petal-fold the flap upward. To do this, lift up one corner while holding down the top of the model just above the horizontal crease and let the sides swing in.

8. Turn the model over.

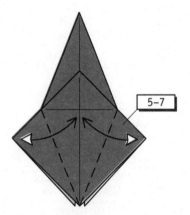 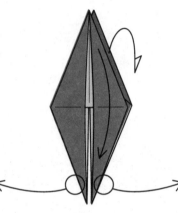 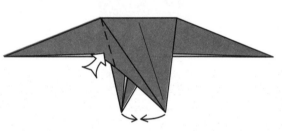

5-7

9. Repeat steps 5–7 on this side.

10. Pull the two bottom flaps as far out to the sides as possible and let the two top flaps swing down in front and behind. The center "hump" should pop down, forming a long valley or groove along the top of the model.

11. Flatten the model completely.

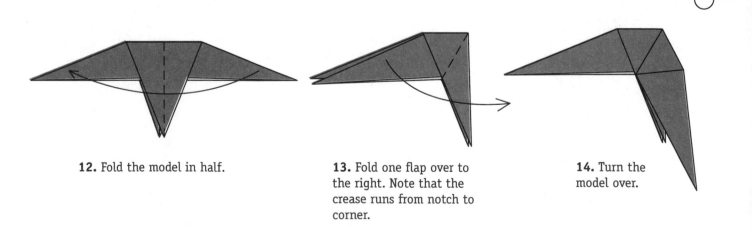

12. Fold the model in half.

13. Fold one flap over to the right. Note that the crease runs from notch to corner.

14. Turn the model over.

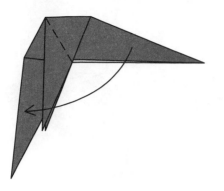

15. Fold the right flap down to match up with the left side.

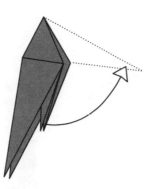

16. Pull one flap out completely.

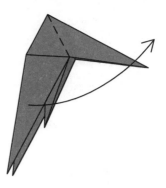

17. Fold one flap up to the right.

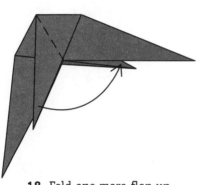

18. Fold one more flap up to the right.

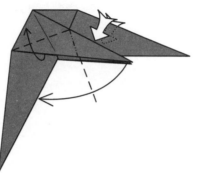

19. Squash-fold the corner down. Repeat behind.

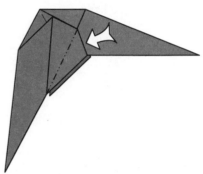

20. Reverse-fold the edge. Repeat behind.

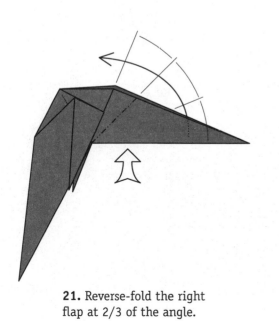

21. Reverse-fold the right flap at 2/3 of the angle.

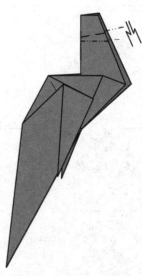

22. Reverse-fold the tip of the flap.

23. Crimp the top flap.

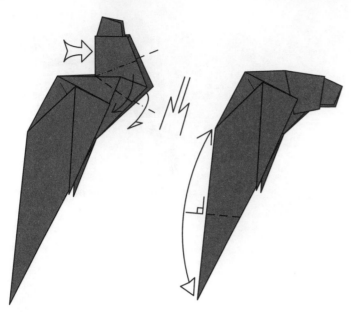

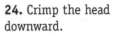

24. Crimp the head downward.

25. Fold and unfold.

26. Fold and unfold.

27. Crimp the tail to the right using the existing creases.

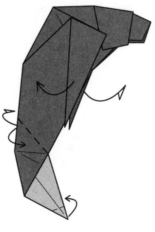

28. Pull out some loose paper in front and behind.

29. Open out the tail and round its tip. Spread the flippers so that they stand straight out from the body.

30. Finished Swimming Manatee. Hold the back and head where shown and pull. The Manatee will swim and wave his flippers.

Kicking Otter

Designed by Robert J. Lang

Combining two action mechanisms in one design, this somewhat difficult model kicks all four limbs. Use a 10 to 12 inch square of thin, crisp paper or foil-backed paper for best results.

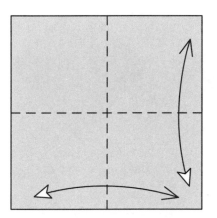

1. Begin with the white side up. Fold the paper in half vertically and horizontally and unfold.

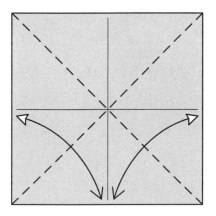

2. Fold and unfold along the diagonals.

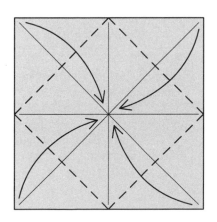

3. Fold the four corners in to the center.

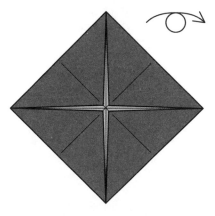

4. Turn the paper over.

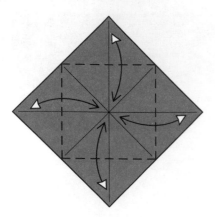

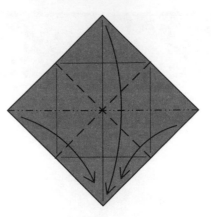

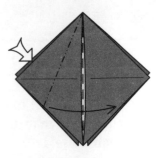

5. Fold all four corners to the center and unfold.

6. Bring all four corners together at the bottom to form a Preliminary Fold.

7. Squash-fold the edge symmetrically.

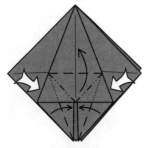

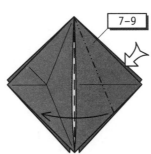

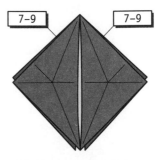

8. Petal-fold the edge.

9. Unfold to step 7.

10. Repeat steps 7–9 on the right.

11. Repeat steps 7–9 on both sides behind.

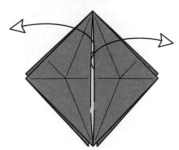

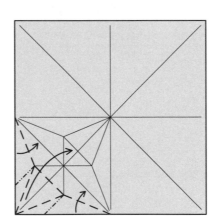

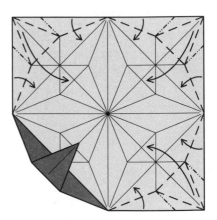

12. Unfold to the original square, white side up.

13. Fold the lower left corner and adjacent edges in toward the center. The valley folds all fall on existing creases, and the mountain folds will form naturally as you flatten the paper.

14. Repeat on the other three corners.

15. Turn the paper over.

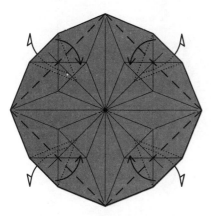
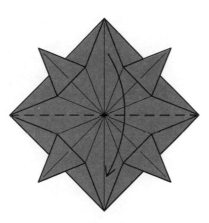
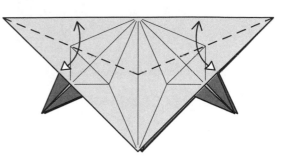

16. Fold four edges in on existing creases, allowing the hidden points to flip out behind.

17. Fold the top half of the paper down to the bottom.

18. Fold and unfold along angle bisectors. Fold only through the near layer.

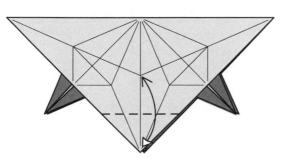
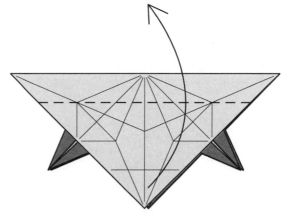

19. Fold the bottom corner up to the crease intersection shown and unfold.

20. Fold the near layer up. Note that the valley fold runs through the intersection of several creases on each side.

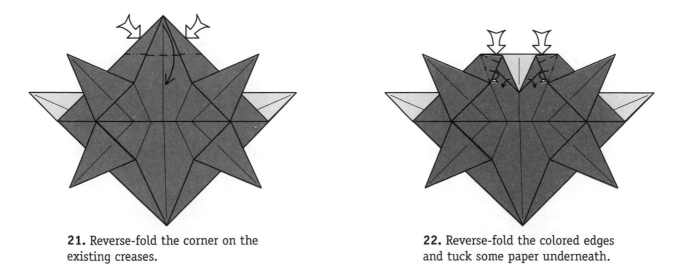

21. Reverse-fold the corner on the existing creases.

22. Reverse-fold the colored edges and tuck some paper underneath.

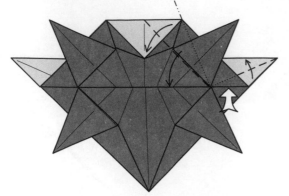

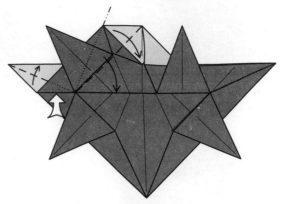

23. Working from the right, swivel the left side of this flap counterclockwise down to the horizontal crease.

24. Repeat step 23 on the left.

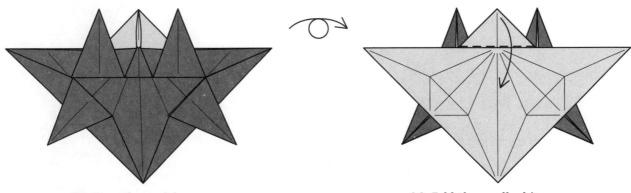

25. Turn the model over.

26. Fold the small white triangular flap at the top down.

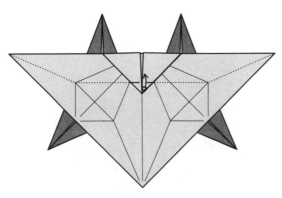

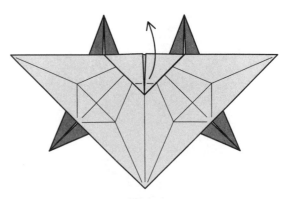

27. Fold the tip of the white triangle and unfold. Note that the crease lines up with a hidden edge.

28. Fold the flap back up.

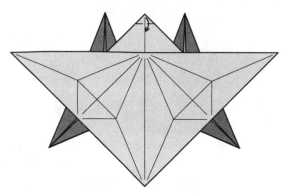

29. Fold the corner down on the crease you just made.

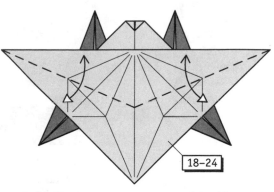

30. Repeat steps 18–24 on this side.

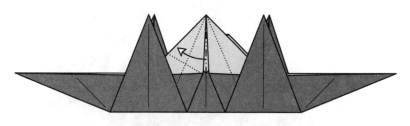

31. Pull out some loose paper and flatten it to the left. Do not repeat behind.

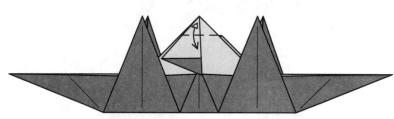

32. Fold and unfold to match up with the edge behind.

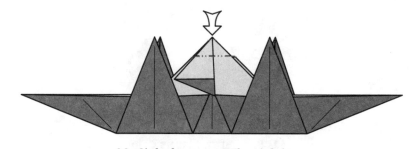

33. Sink the corner. The sink is partially closed, but the near flap on the left should swing freely from left to right.

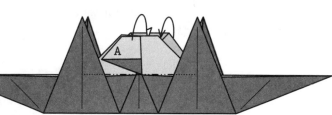

34. Fold both white flaps into the interior of the model. Slip flap A into the corresponding pocket on the far flap and flatten the model.

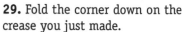

35. Fold and unfold lightly through all layers.

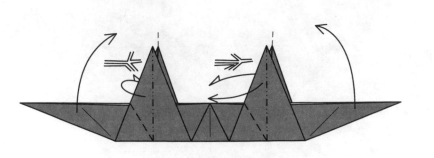

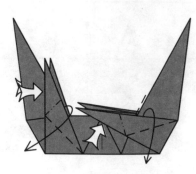

36. Crimp using the creases you just made. Although there is an odd number of layers, make the crimp nearly symmetric from front to back.

37. Squash-fold all four points.

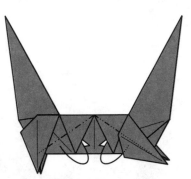

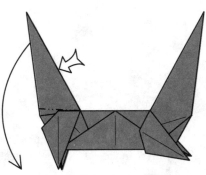

38. Mountain-fold the corners into the pockets. Repeat behind.

39. Reverse-fold the point down as far as possible.

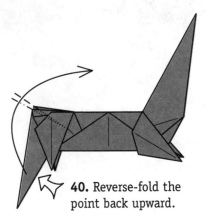

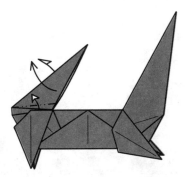

40. Reverse-fold the point back upward.

41. Pull out two layers of loose paper, one colored and one white. Repeat behind.

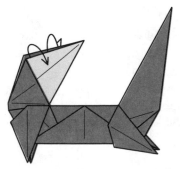

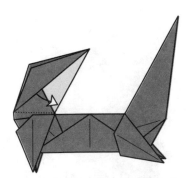

42. Open the flap from the left and wrap one inner layer around to the front. Repeat behind.

43. Pull out a single layer of paper. Repeat behind.

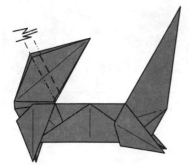

44. Crimp the point in and out.

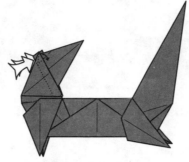

45. Reverse-fold the corner. Repeat behind.

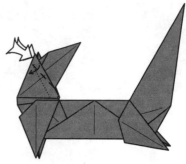

46. Squash-fold the corner. Repeat behind.

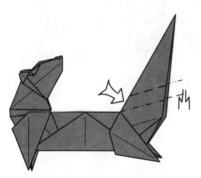

47. Valley-fold the corner up. Repeat behind.

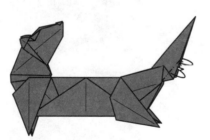

48. Reverse-fold the tip of the nose.

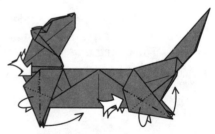

49. Squash-fold the tip of the nose and wrap its edges downward.

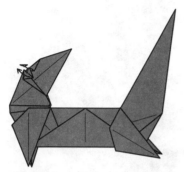

50. Crimp the tail.

51. Mountain-fold the corners inside.

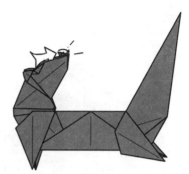

52. Mountain-fold the four legs in half (at 90°) and lift them up so that they stand out from the body. Pinch the base of each leg so that it stands straight out.

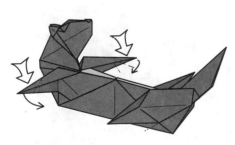

53. Squash-fold the forepaws.

54. Crimp the hind feet.

55. Finished Kicking Otter. Pull on the neck and tail (either together or singly). The Otter will kick his front and back feet.

Tyrannosaurus Rex

Designed by Robert J. Lang

This is a very difficult model! You should use thin, crisp paper or foil-backed paper and for your first try, should use a square at least 10 to 12 inches in size.

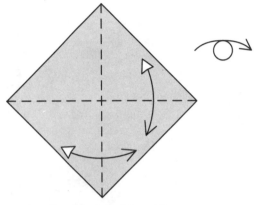

1. Begin with the white side up. Fold the paper in half along the diagonals and unfold. Turn the paper over.

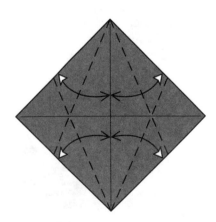

2. Fold each edge in turn to lie along the vertical center crease and unfold.

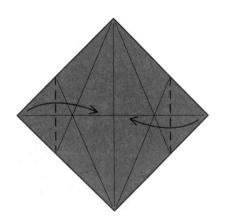

3. Fold the side corners in. Note that the creases hit the edge at existing creases.

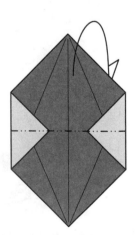

4. Mountain-fold the top half of the model behind.

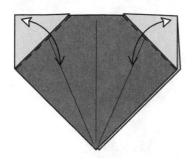

5. Fold and unfold along the raw edge.

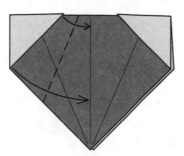

6. Fold the white corner down so that the raw edge lines up with the vertical crease.

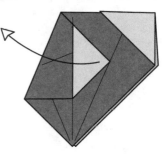

7. Unfold.

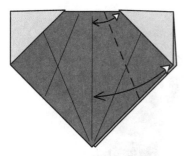

8. Repeat steps 6–7 on the right.

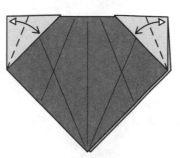

9. Fold and unfold.

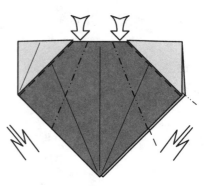

10. Crimp on existing creases.

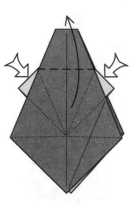

11. Petal-fold, pushing in the white layers.

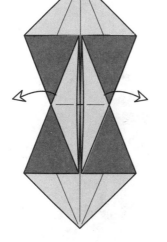

12. Loosen the model and pull out the white corners that are trapped inside.

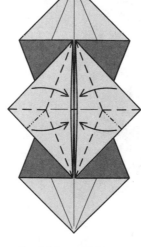

13. Fold a rabbit ear from each side.

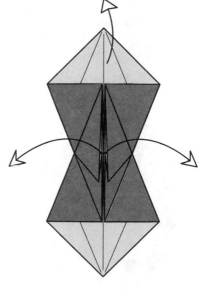

14. Open out the model, leaving the rabbit ears in place.

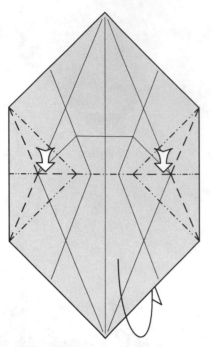

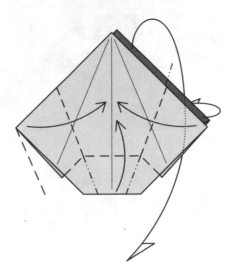

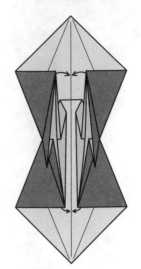

15. Mountain-fold the bottom up behind and push in the sides using existing creases.

16. Fold the bottom up, the sides in, and swing the top far flap down behind.

17. Flatten the model.

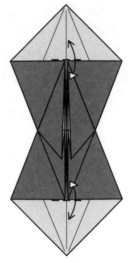

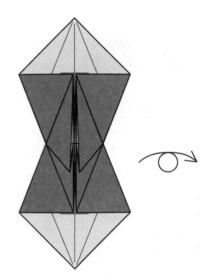

18. Fold and unfold, forming two pinch marks.

19. Turn the paper over.

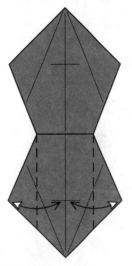

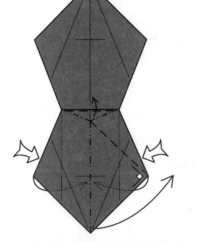

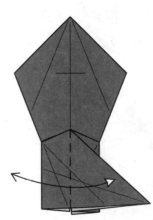

20. Fold the side corners in to the center line and unfold.

21. Push the sides in; pinch the bottom point in half and swing it over to the right. The vertical x-ray lines indicate valley folds on the hidden layers.

22. Fold the flap to the left and unfold.

23. Fold and unfold.

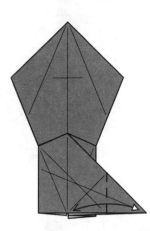

24. Fold and unfold.

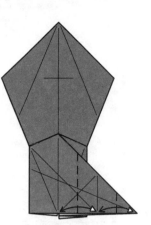

25. Fold and unfold, dividing the flap into fourths.

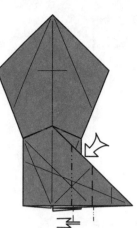

26. Reverse-fold in and out.

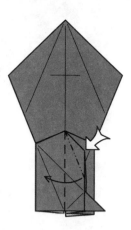

27. Spread-sink the corner symmetrically.

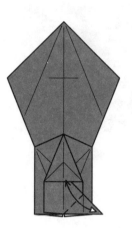

28. Fold and unfold.

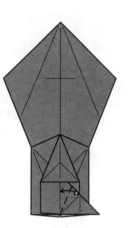

29. Fold and unfold.

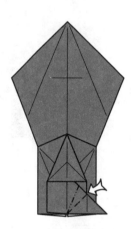

30. Reverse-fold in and out on the creases you just made.

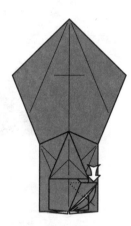

31. Reverse-fold the corner down to the bottom of the model.

32. Spread-sink the corner, spreading the layers at the bottom symmetrically.

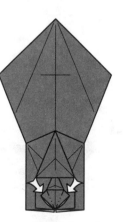

33. Reverse-fold the edges.

34. Fold the blunt corner downward.

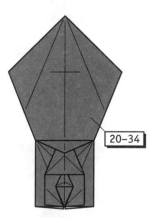

20–34

35. Repeat steps 20–34 on the top.

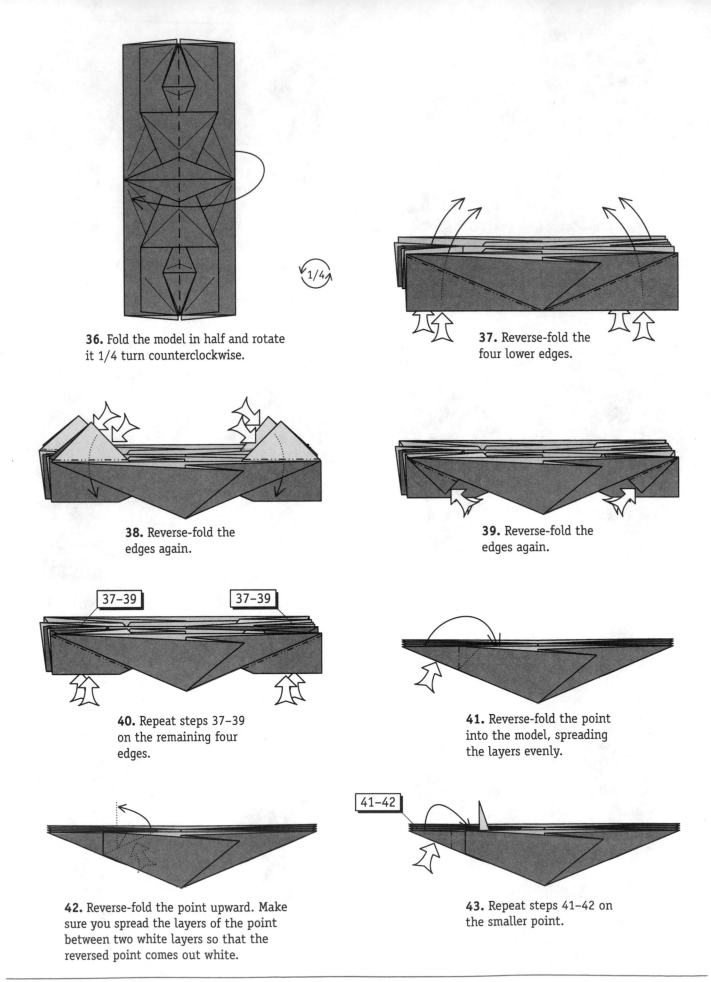

36. Fold the model in half and rotate it 1/4 turn counterclockwise.

37. Reverse-fold the four lower edges.

38. Reverse-fold the edges again.

39. Reverse-fold the edges again.

37–39   37–39

40. Repeat steps 37–39 on the remaining four edges.

41. Reverse-fold the point into the model, spreading the layers evenly.

42. Reverse-fold the point upward. Make sure you spread the layers of the point between two white layers so that the reversed point comes out white.

41–42

43. Repeat steps 41–42 on the smaller point.

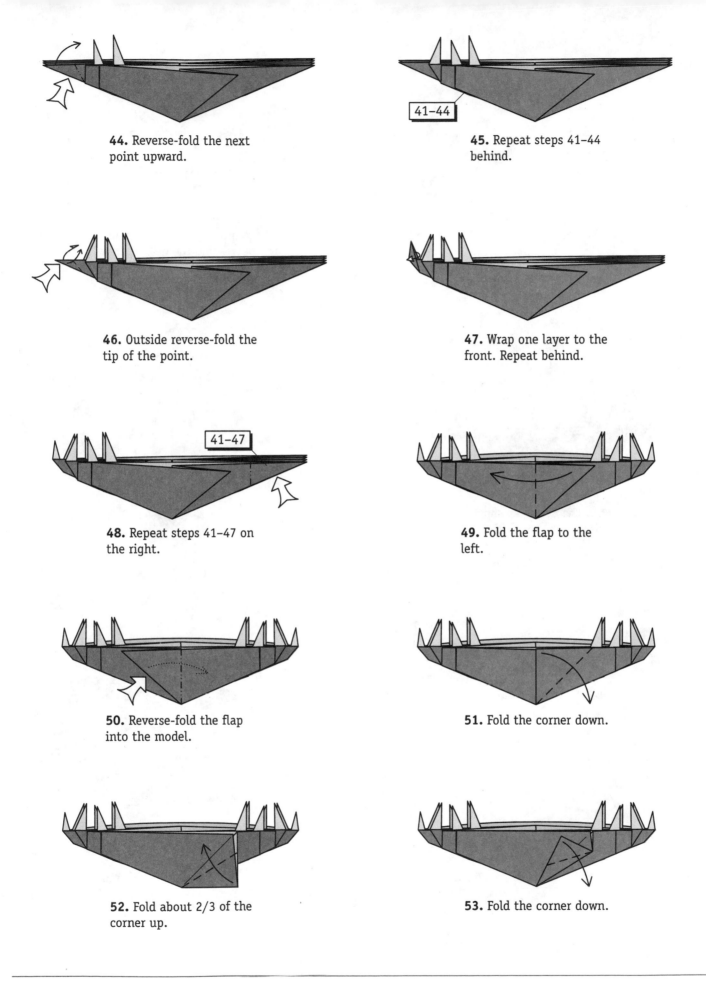

44. Reverse-fold the next point upward.

45. Repeat steps 41–44 behind.

41–44

46. Outside reverse-fold the tip of the point.

47. Wrap one layer to the front. Repeat behind.

41–47

48. Repeat steps 41–47 on the right.

49. Fold the flap to the left.

50. Reverse-fold the flap into the model.

51. Fold the corner down.

52. Fold about 2/3 of the corner up.

53. Fold the corner down.

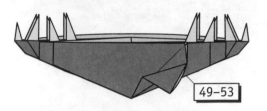

54. Repeat steps 49–53 behind.

55. Squash the middle white layer symmetrically, spreading the near and far layers apart (see step 57).

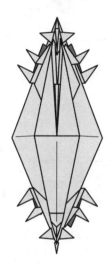

56. The next step shows a view of the top of the model.

57. Like this.

58. Pinch all of the teeth. Round the eyes.

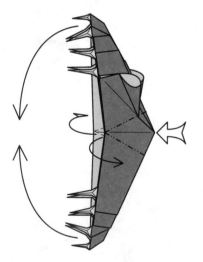

59. Pinch mountain folds through all layers where shown; swing the jaws together and bring the sides of the mouth to the right. The corners will overlap in the middle.

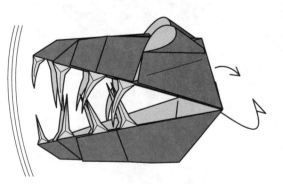

60. Finished Tyrannosaurus Rex. Squeeze the sides of the jaws and he will open and close his mouth.

Indian Paddling a Canoe

Designed by Robert J. Lang

Despite the complexity of this model, if you look close, you'll see that the action mechanism is the same as that in Randlett's Flapping Bird! Use a 10 to 12 inch square of thin paper.

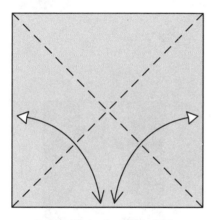

1. Begin with the white side up. Fold and unfold along the diagonals.

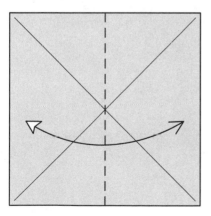

2. Fold the paper in half vertically and unfold.

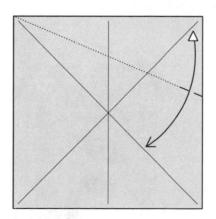

3. Fold the top edge down to lie along the diagonal, but make the crease sharp only where it hits the right edge.

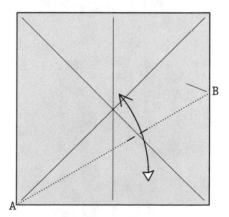

4. Make a crease that runs between points A and B, but make it sharp only where it crosses the diagonal.

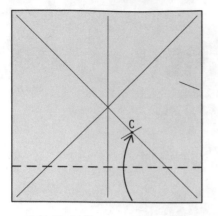 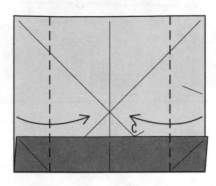 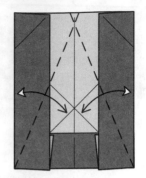

5. Fold the bottom edge up to touch point C.

6. Fold the side edges in. Note that the creases hit the bottom edge at the same point as the diagonal creases (also, the right edge touches point C).

7. Fold the left side edge in to lie along the diagonal and unfold. Repeat on the right.

  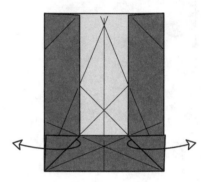

8. Fold the bottom corners out to the sides.

9. Fold the bottom edge to the diagonal creases and unfold.

10. Pull the loose corners out to the sides.

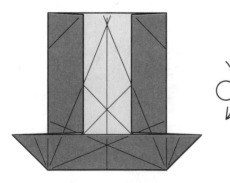 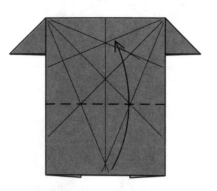

11. Turn the paper over from top to bottom.

12. Fold the bottom edge up. Note that the crease runs through the intersection of existing creases.

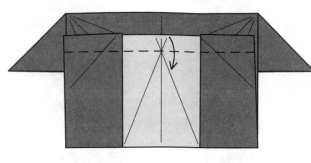

13. Fold the raw edge down along a crease that runs through the intersection of two creases.

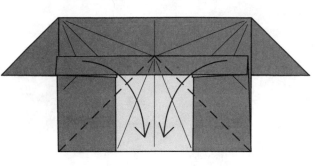

14. Fold two corners to meet at the bottom.

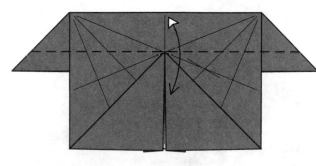

15. Fold and unfold.

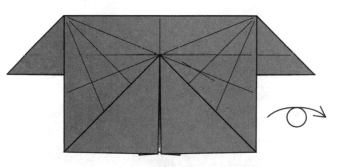

16. Turn the model over.

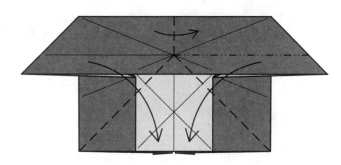

17. Fold a rabbit ear.

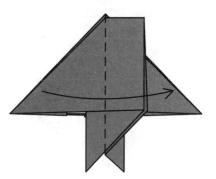

18. Fold the model in half.

19. Fold one flap down to align with the left edge. Repeat behind.

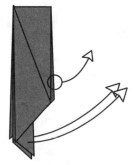

20. Hold gently at the left and put the central layers out, rotating them counterclockwise.

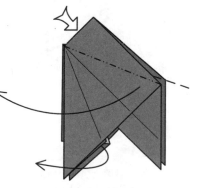

21. Swing the near flap to the left, squash-folding the top flap downward.

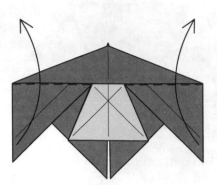

22. Fold two flaps up as far as possible.

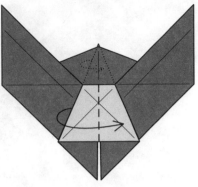

23. Fold one flap to the right.

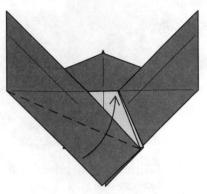

24. Fold one flap up.

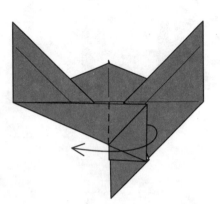

25. Fold one flap back to the left.

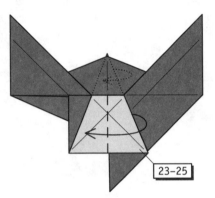

26. Repeat steps 23–25 on the right.

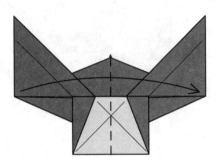

27. Fold the model in half.

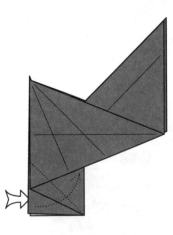

28. Reverse-fold the white flap upward so that its edges line up with the existing vertical edges.

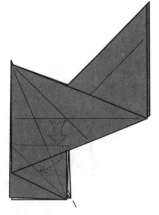

29. Reverse-fold the hidden white flap again to line up with the edges of the reverse fold you just made.

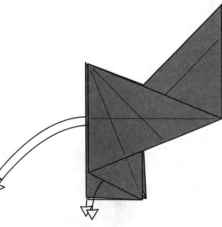

30. Loosen the layers along the left side so that you can pull out the large central flap.

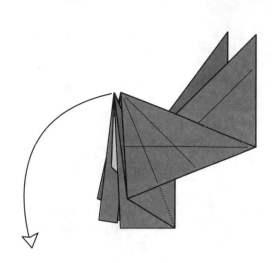

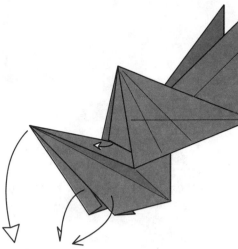

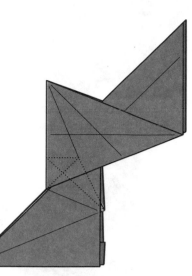

31. Pull the central flap out and downward from the trapped layers.

32. In progress. Pull the central flap all the way down, freeing some trapped paper in the middle and bringing the two loose flaps at the bottom together.

33. The hidden lines show the edges of the white layer inside.

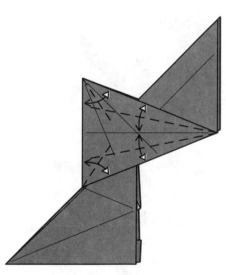

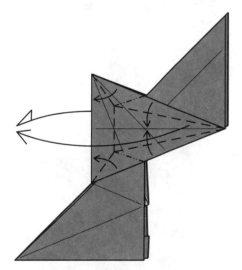

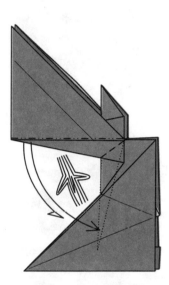

34. Fold and unfold along four angle bisectors. Repeat behind.

35. Fold a rabbit ear at the top and bottom of the flap and swing the flap over to the left. Repeat behind.

36. Crimp the top of the model downward. The side view shows the distribution of layers in the crimp. Note that the middle layer crimp stays in the middle.

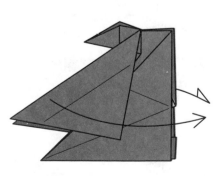

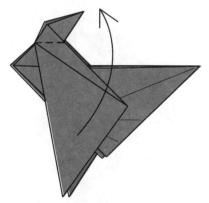

37. Fold one flap to the right in front and behind.

38. Turn the model over and rotate it 1/8 turn clockwise.

39. Fold one flap up in front. Do not repeat behind.

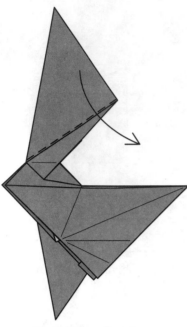

40. Fold one flap down.

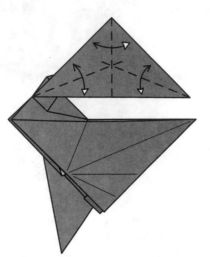

41. Fold and unfold.

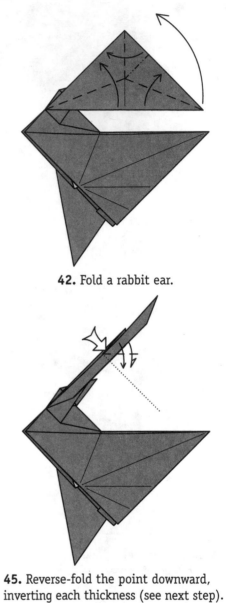

42. Fold a rabbit ear.

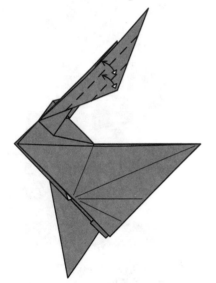

43. Fold and unfold in thirds.

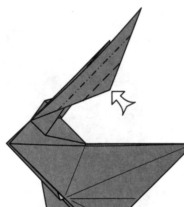

44. Open-sink in and out using the creases you just made.

45. Reverse-fold the point downward, inverting each thickness (see next step).

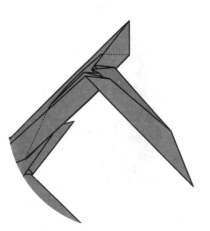

46. Close-up view of the reverse fold. Flatten.

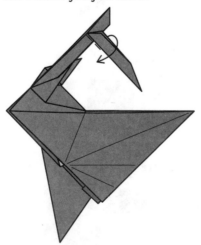

47. Fold the flap down and to the left.

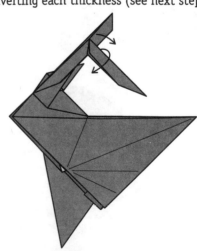

48. Working from the right, open out one contiguous edge.

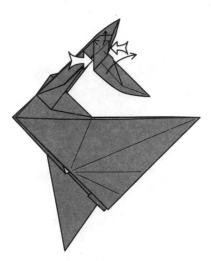

49. Squash the top of the flap over to the left.

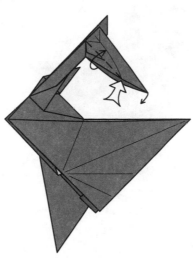

50. Push the corner inside-out and fold the left side of the flap over to the right.

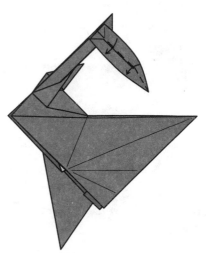

51. Close up the flap.

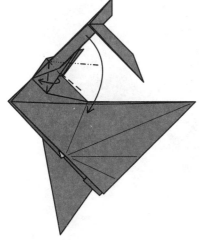

52. Crimp the arm downward.

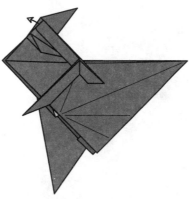

53. Pull out some loose paper behind the shoulder. Valley-fold the narrow flap underneath the arm.

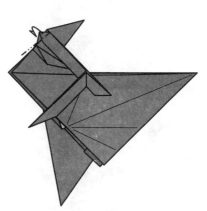

54. Mountain-fold the paper into the interior of the model.

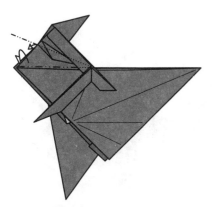

55. Mountain-fold the edge, pulling down as much loose paper from the interior of the man as possible.

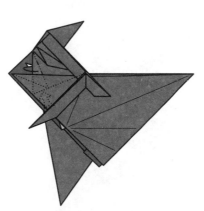

56. Swivel-fold the left edge of the model and tuck the extra paper into a white pocket.

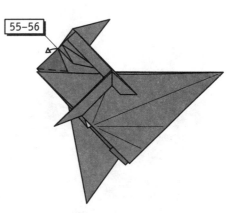

57. Repeat steps 55–56 behind.

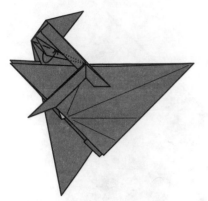

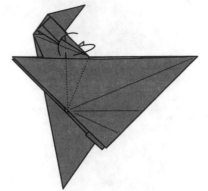

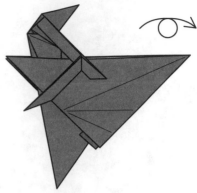

58. Fold a narrow flap upward as far as possible.

59. One arm is not shown in this view. Fold the flap into the central pocket.

60. Turn the model over.

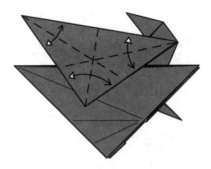

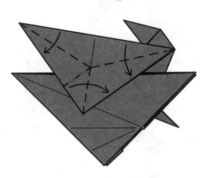

61. Fold the flap up.

62. Fold and unfold.

63. Fold a rabbit ear from the flap.

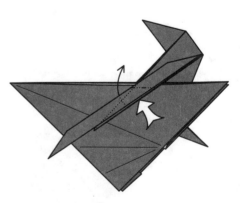

64. Crease into thirds.

65. Open-sink in and out on the creases you just made.

66. Reverse-fold the point upward, dividing the layers between the layers of the triangular point (whose edge is shown by a hidden line).

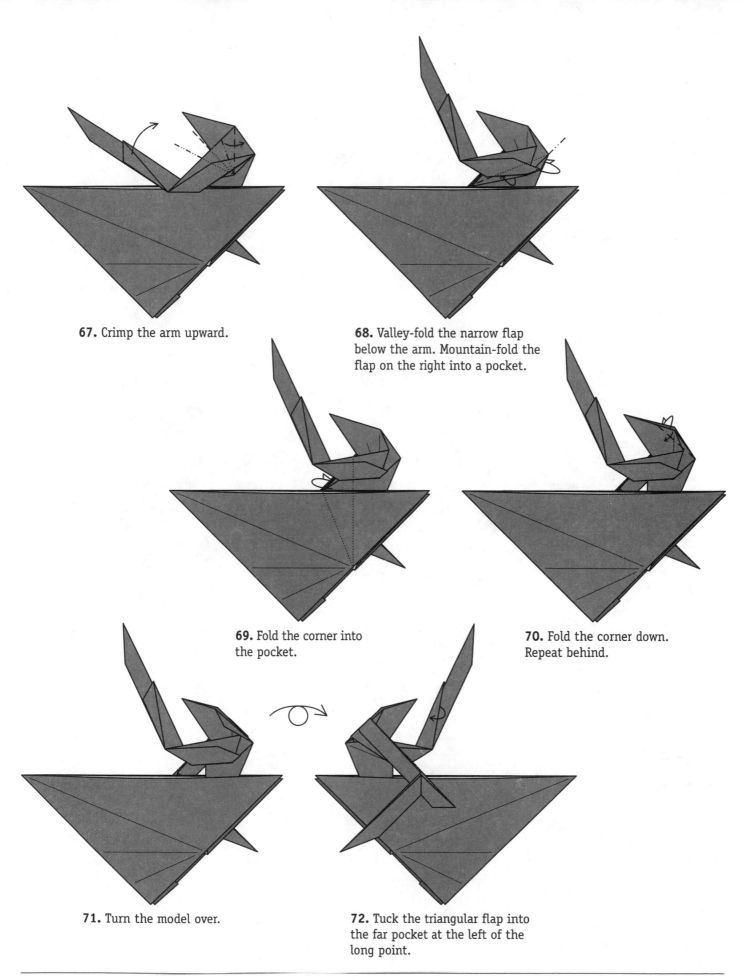

67. Crimp the arm upward.

68. Valley-fold the narrow flap below the arm. Mountain-fold the flap on the right into a pocket.

69. Fold the corner into the pocket.

70. Fold the corner down. Repeat behind.

71. Turn the model over.

72. Tuck the triangular flap into the far pocket at the left of the long point.

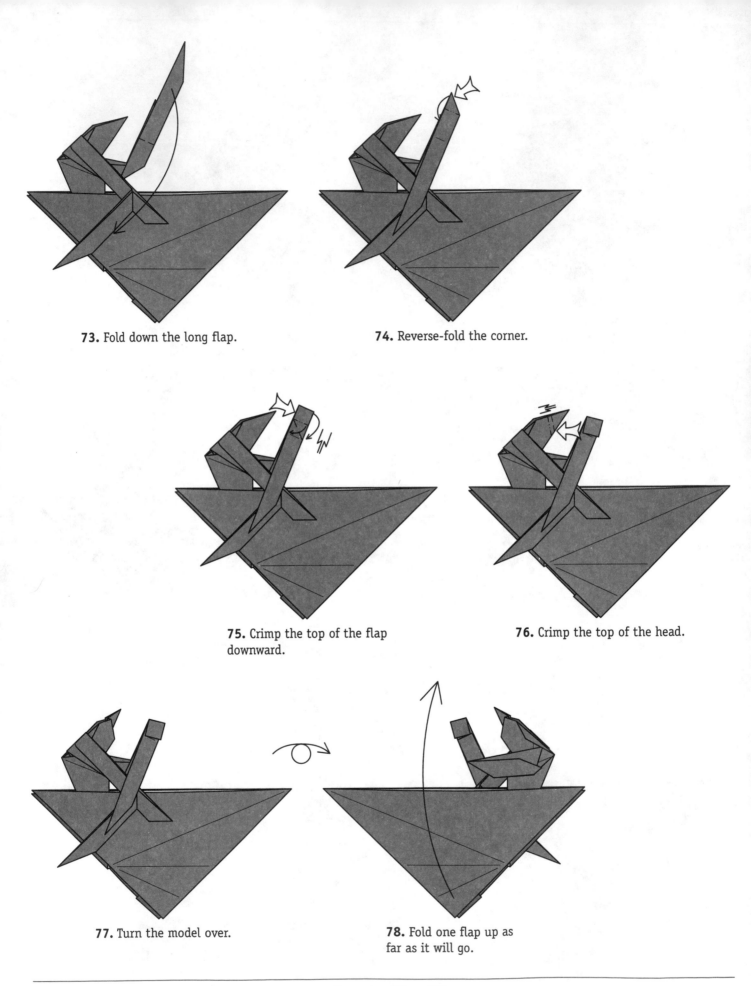

73. Fold down the long flap.

74. Reverse-fold the corner.

75. Crimp the top of the flap downward.

76. Crimp the top of the head.

77. Turn the model over.

78. Fold one flap up as far as it will go.

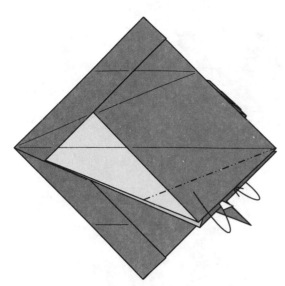

79. Mountain-fold two corners inside.

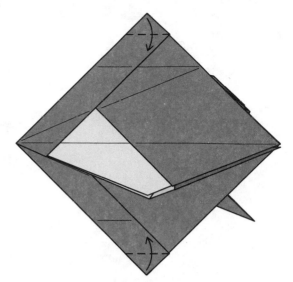

80. Valley-fold the top and bottom corners.

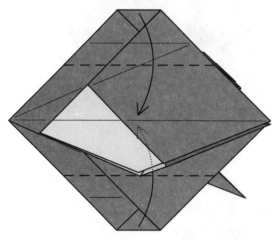

81. Valley-fold the top and bottom edges to the horizontal center line.

82. Fold one layer down.

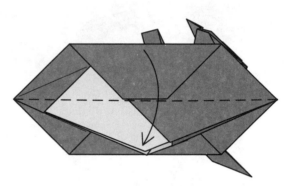

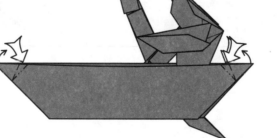

83. Crimp both ends of the canoe.

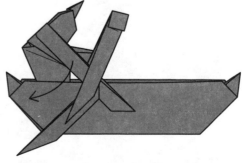

84. Turn the model over.

85. Pull the near arm out to stand straight out from the body.

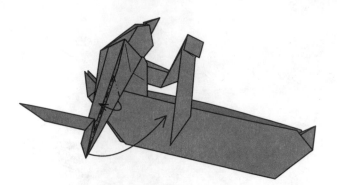

86. Reverse-fold the arm to the right.

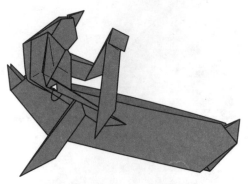

87. Tuck the triangular edge inside the layers of the forearm.

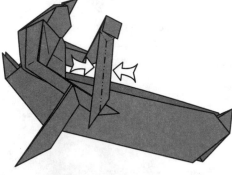

88. Pinch the right flap.

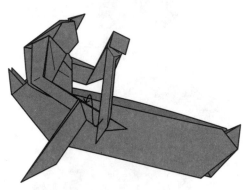

89. Tuck the point into the pocket in the paddle.

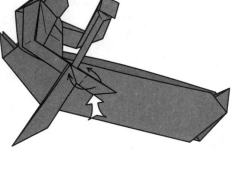

90. Outside reverse-fold the hand back over the paddle.

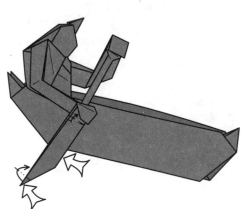

91. Crimp and squash the paddle slightly. Reverse-fold its tip.

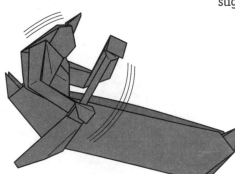

92. Finished Indian Paddling a Canoe. Pull his head and he paddles.

Strumming Guitarist

Designed by Robert J. Lang

This model uses the same mechanism as the Indian Paddling a Canoe. You can adapt it to make a quite a few different instrumentalists. Use a 10 to 12 inch square for your first attempt.

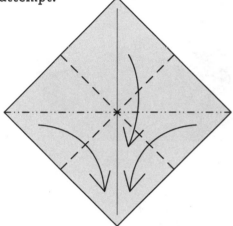

1. Fold a Preliminary Fold.

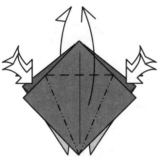

2. Petal-fold both sides to make a Bird Base.

3. Unfold completely.

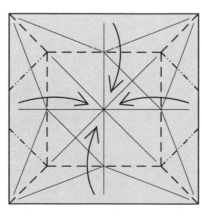

4. Fold in the edges all the way around and rabbit-ear the corners.

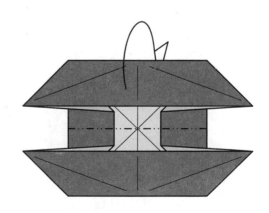

5. Mountain-fold in half.

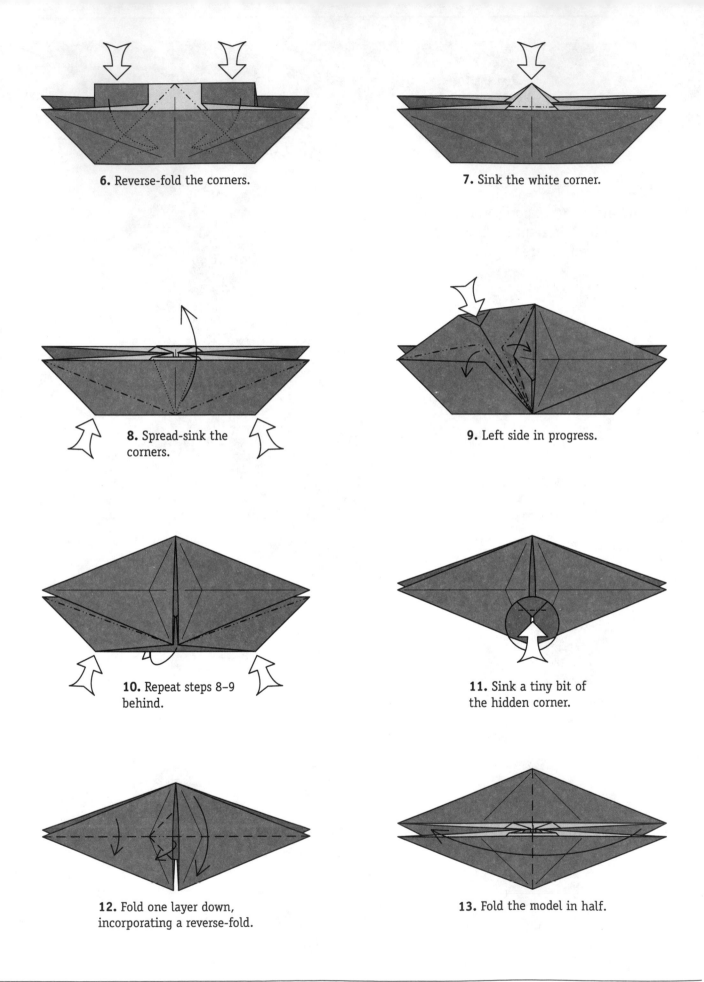

6. Reverse-fold the corners.

7. Sink the white corner.

8. Spread-sink the corners.

9. Left side in progress.

10. Repeat steps 8–9 behind.

11. Sink a tiny bit of the hidden corner.

12. Fold one layer down, incorporating a reverse-fold.

13. Fold the model in half.

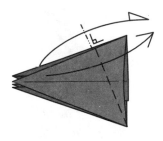

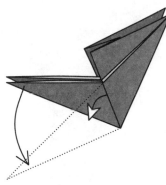

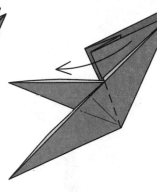

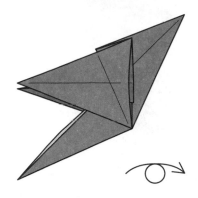

14. Fold one flap upward in front and behind.

15. Pull one flap downward, releasing some loose paper.

16. Fold one flap back to the left.

17. Turn the model over.

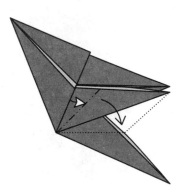

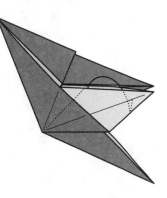

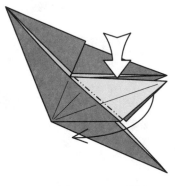

18. Pull out some loose paper.

19. Pull out the same amount of paper behind.

20. Reverse-fold the white corner.

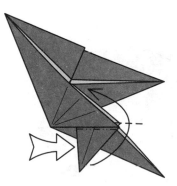

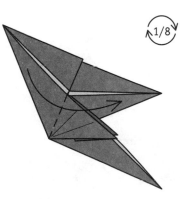

21. Reverse-fold the corner.

22. Fold one layer down and rotate the model 1/8 turn clockwise.

23. Fold and unfold; repeat behind.

24. Form a rabbit ear at top and bottom and swing the flap up to the left; repeat behind.

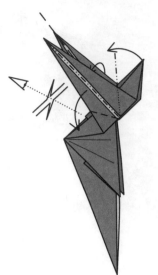

25. Crimp the model asymmetrically. Note how one side goes up and the other goes down when viewed edge-on.

26. Mountain-fold the corners.

27. Turn the model over.

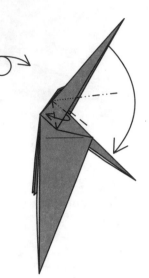

28. Crimp the flap down asymmetrically.

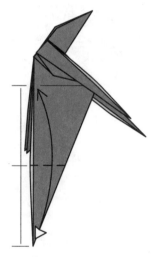

29. Fold and unfold.

30. Fold upward the corner that is partially hidden by the near arm.

31. Mountain-fold the corner to the inside.

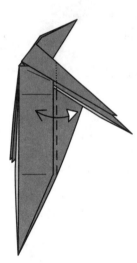

32. Fold and unfold through all layers.

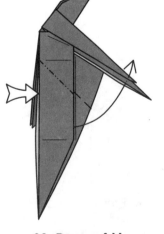

33. Reverse-fold.

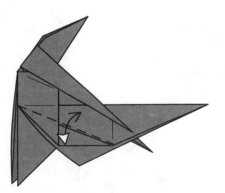

34. Crease through both layers.

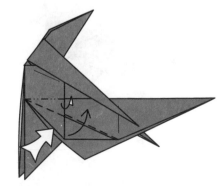

35. Reverse-fold the corner.

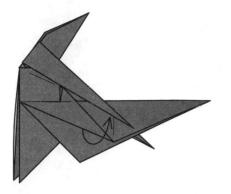

36. Loosen the paper and wrap one layer to the front.

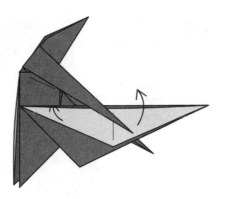

37. Fold the white layer up and tuck it under the flap at the body.

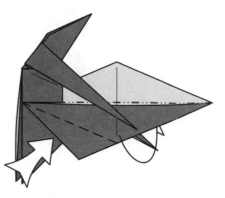

38. Reverse-fold the edge.

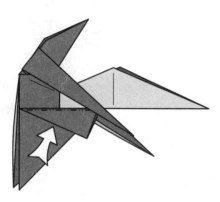

39. Reverse-fold the edge.

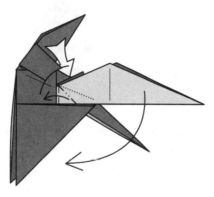

40. The near arm is cut away in this view to show the layers behind it. Swivel the white flap down.

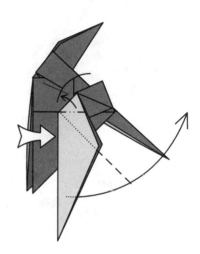

41. Squash-fold the flap upward.

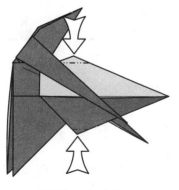

42. Closed-sink the two corners.

43. Reverse-fold about 1/3 of the point.

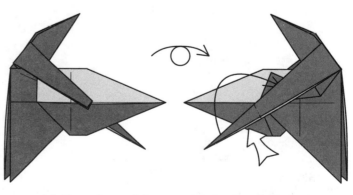

44. Turn the model over.

45. Reverse-fold about 2/5 of the point.

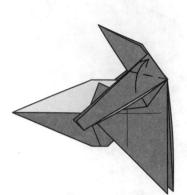

46. Fold the flap upward.

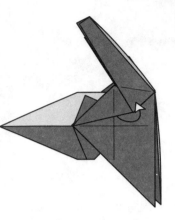

47. Bring one layer in front of the blunt flap, turning it inside-out.

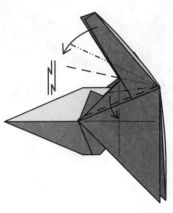

48. Crimp the arm downward.

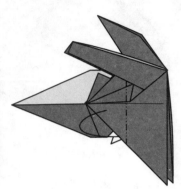

49. Mountain-fold the triangle inside.

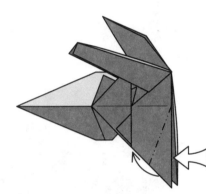

50. Reverse-fold the leg to the left so its edge lines up with the corner.

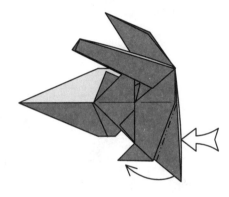

51. Repeat step 50 behind.

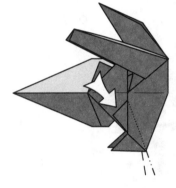

52. Reverse-fold the corner.

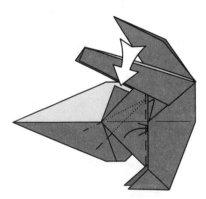

53. Squash-fold and tuck the resulting flap inside the body.

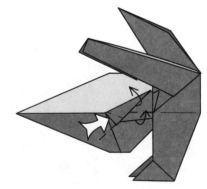

54. Swivel-fold and squash-fold so that the bottom edge is horizontal.

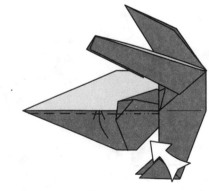

55. Reverse-fold the colored flap up inside the white one.

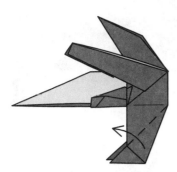

56. Fold one layer of the foot upward.

57. Wrap a single layer of paper around the other flap; repeat steps 56–57 behind.

58. Turn the model over.

59. Reverse-fold the top of the head.

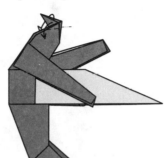

60. Outside-reverse-fold the hair.

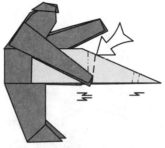

61. Crimp the guitar (the white flap) halfway down the flap and pleat its tip.

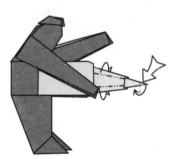

62. Blunt the tip of the guitar with a small reverse fold; narrow the neck with mountain folds.

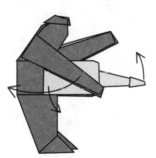

63. Pull the near arm over to stand straight out from the body. Rotate the guitar away from you and twist its neck slightly upward.

64. Reverse-fold the left arm to curl around the guitar. Fold the right arm down and wrap the edges of the hand around the neck of the guitar.

65. Outside reverse-fold the arm.

66. Carefully tuck the corner of the arm under a single layer of paper. Squash-fold the hand. Shape the guitar.

67. Finished Strumming Guitarist. Hold the back and pull the head, and he will strum the guitar.

Fiddling Bassist

Designed by Robert J. Lang

This is a very difficult model. Use a square of thin paper or foil-backed paper at least 12 inches on a side for your first attempt.

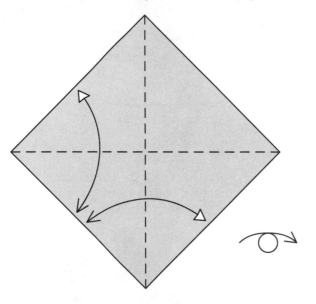

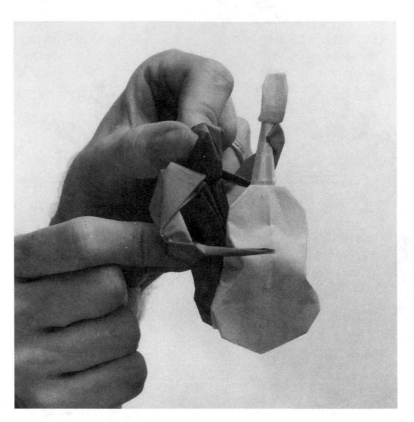

1. Begin with the white side up. Fold and unfold along the diagonals. Turn the paper over.

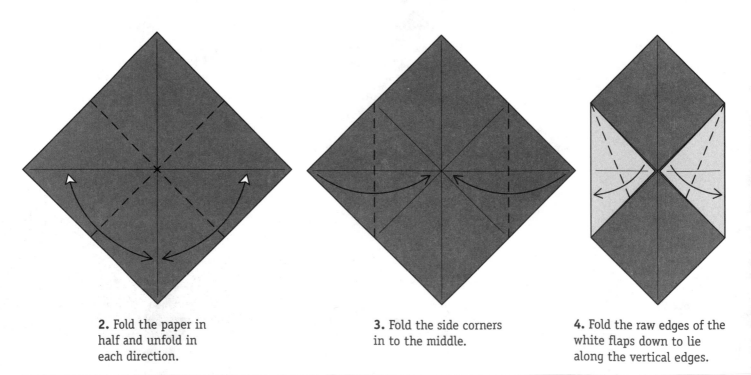

2. Fold the paper in half and unfold in each direction.

3. Fold the side corners in to the middle.

4. Fold the raw edges of the white flaps down to lie along the vertical edges.

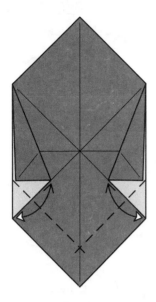

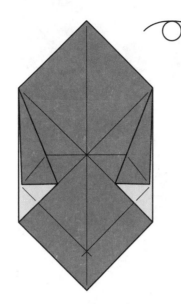

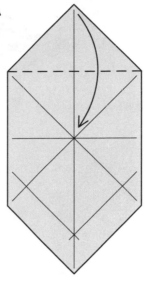

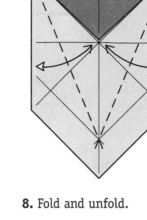

5. Fold and unfold.

6. Turn the model over.

7. Fold the top corner down.

8. Fold and unfold.

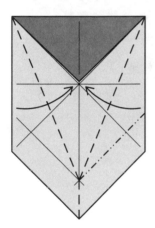

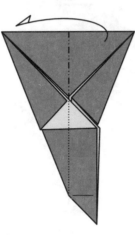

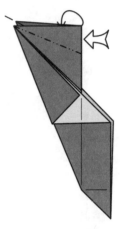

9. Fold a rabbit ear using the existing creases.

10. Swing the right side behind and to the left.

11. Fold and unfold.

12. Reverse-fold the corner inside.

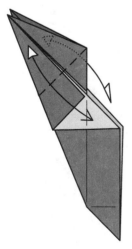

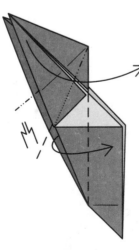

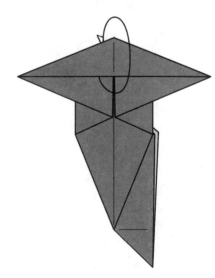

13. Fold and unfold. Repeat behind.

14. Crimp the upper left layers downward.

15. Swing one flap over to the right.

16. Wrap one layer from front to back.

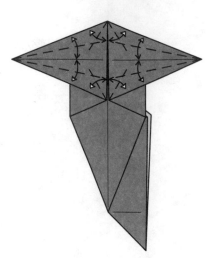

17. Fold and unfold along the angle bisectors.

18. Turn the model over.

19. Fold the left flap down to the right in front and let its hidden lower corner flip up behind.

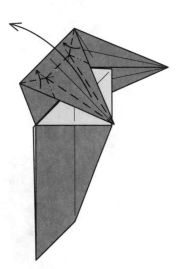

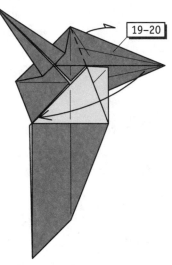

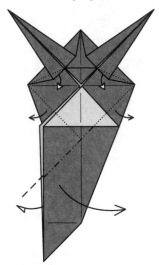

20. Narrow the flap with rabbit ears using the existing creases.

21. Repeat steps 19–20 on the right.

22. Pull some trapped paper out from under the two skinny points at the top and open out the bottom.

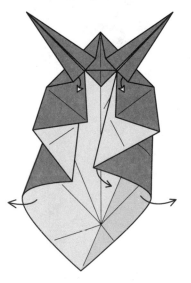

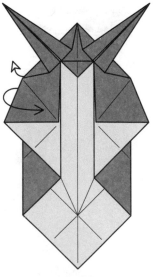

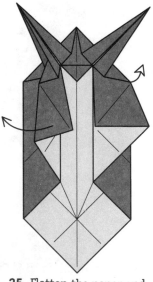

23. In progress.

24. Separate the near and far layers at the left.

25. Flatten the paper and repeat on the right.

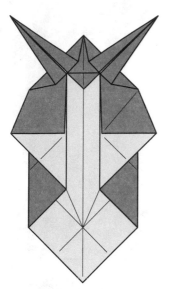

26. Turn the model over.

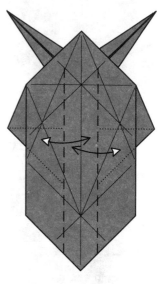

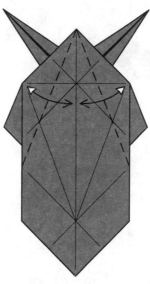

27. Fold and unfold through all layers.

28. Fold and unfold. The creases line up with folded edges behind.

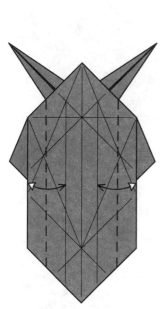

29. Fold and unfold through the near layers.

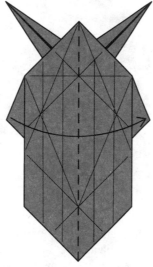

30. Fold the model in half.

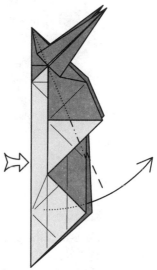

31. Reverse-fold the bottom of the model.

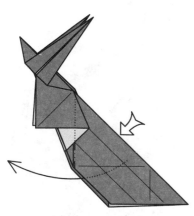

32. Reverse-fold the bottom point to the left.

33. Pull out some loose paper. Repeat behind.

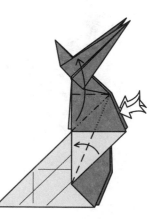

34. Squash-fold the edge. Repeat behind.

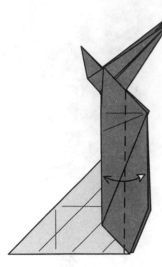

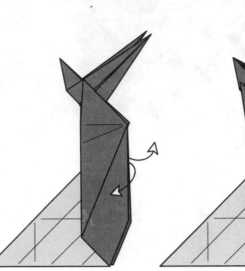

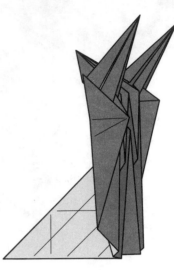

35. Fold and unfold through all layers.

36. Spread the edges along the right side.

37. This is a complex sink. The two corners marked with a C are closed sinks; all of the other corners are open-sunk. They all have to be inverted together.

38. The result. Flatten the model.

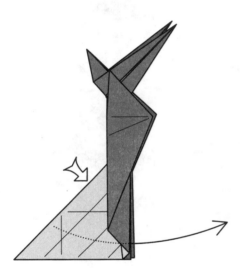

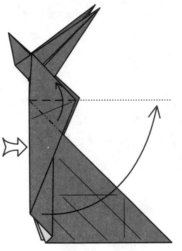

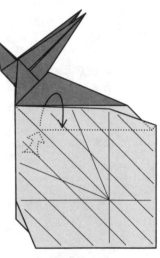

39. Reverse-fold the point all the way to the right (you're actually undoing part of the sink from step 37).

40. Open the lower half of the model diagonally upward, swivelling the colored flap upward counterclockwise.

41. Closed-sink the hidden corner upward and bring two layers of paper to the front.

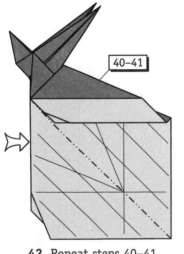

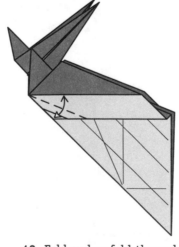

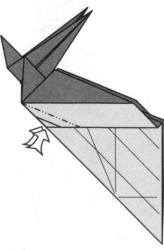

42. Repeat steps 40–41 behind.

43. Fold and unfold through the thick flap. Repeat behind.

44. Open-sink the corner. Repeat behind.

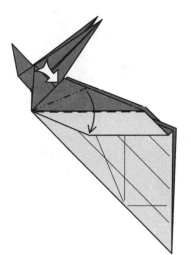

45. Squash-fold the edge.

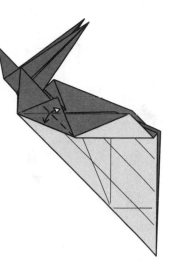

46. Fold and unfold through the near flap only.

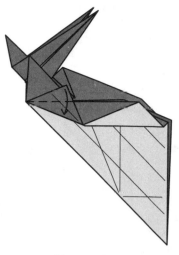

47. Fold one edge down.

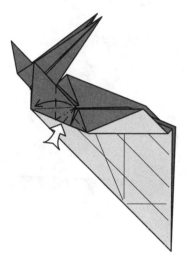

48. Stretch the corner over to the left edge.

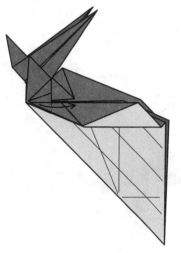

49. Fold the corner back to the right.

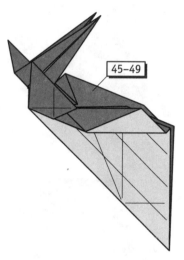

45–49

50. Repeat steps 45–49 behind.

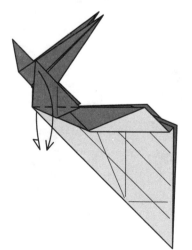

51. Fold two flaps down.

52. Crimp the head and arms over to the right. The extra layer in the middle should go with the far layer.

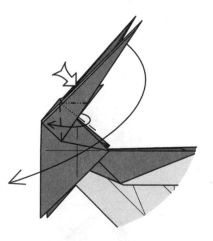

53. Fold one edge to the left and squash-fold the point down to the lower left. Do not repeat behind.

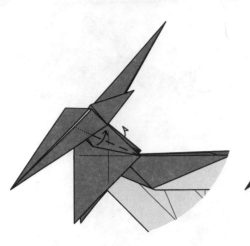

54. Fold the narrow edge upward. Repeat behind.

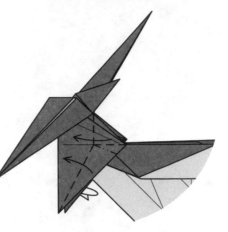

55. Fold a rabbit ear. Repeat behind.

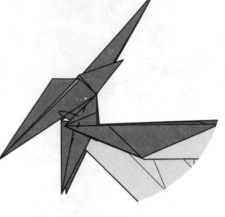

56. Mountain-fold the corner behind. Repeat behind.

57. Mountain-fold the edge of the head. Repeat behind.

58. Reverse-fold the top of the head.

59. Outside reverse-fold the top of the head.

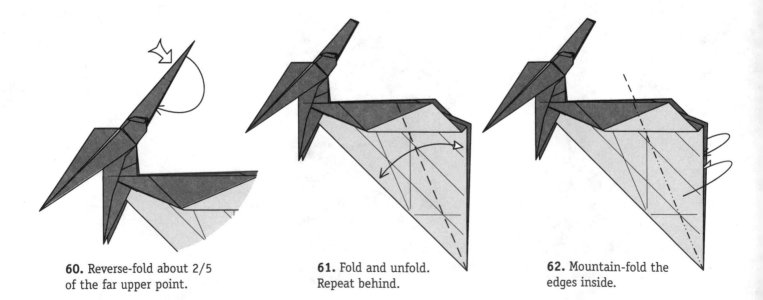

60. Reverse-fold about 2/5 of the far upper point.

61. Fold and unfold. Repeat behind.

62. Mountain-fold the edges inside.

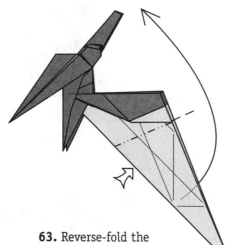

63. Reverse-fold the white point upward.

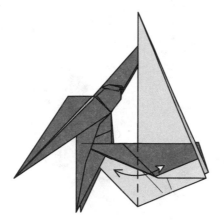

64. Fold and unfold; repeat behind.

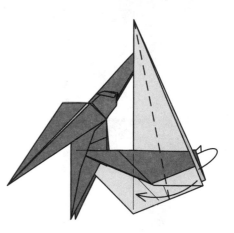

65. Valley-fold the near edge to line up with the vertical folded edge. Repeat behind.

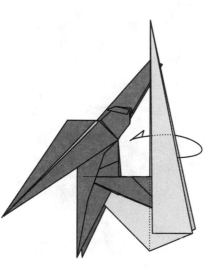

66. Swing the far edge of the vertical white flap behind and flatten.

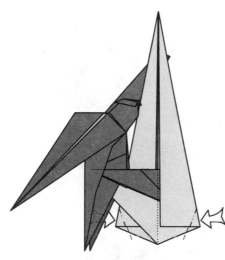

67. Reverse-fold the bottom corners.

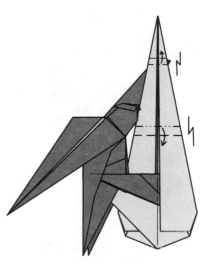

68. Pleat the white flap.

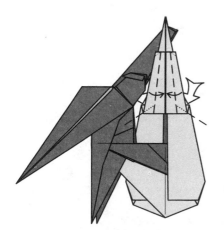

69. Valley-fold the edges of the neck of the bass in to the center; collars will form at the bottom as the neck is flattened.

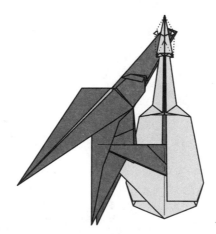

70. Pull out some paper at the top of the neck.

71. Crimp the upraised hand. Outside reverse-fold the feet.

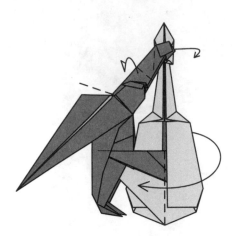

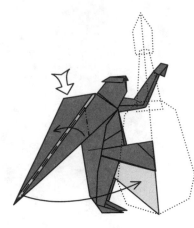

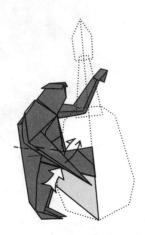

72. Swing the bass around to the front. Bend the far arm down and curve it around so that the hand rests on the neck of the bass.

73. Reverse-fold the near arm underneath.

74. Outside reverse-fold the arm.

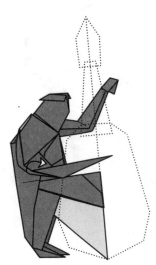

75. Tuck the upper layer of the arm into the pocket in the lower layer.

76. Pinch the point to make a bow.

77. Curve the left hand around and wrap it around the neck of the bass.

78. Shape the bass and position it to the player.

79. Finished Fiddling Bassist. Hold his back and pull his head and he will fiddle the bass.

Flasher

Designed by Jeremy Shafer and Chris Palmer

The joint designers of this model call it a "hyper-action" model. Chris Palmer and Jeremy Shafer have devised whole families of twisted springy designs, including decorations, opening flowers, and self-propelled tops. This model is based on a technique by Toshikazu Kawasaki that he calls "iso-area twist folding." Use a 12 inch or larger square of very springy paper for the best results.

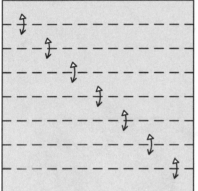

1. With the white side up, divide the paper into eighths by folding it first in half, then in quarters and then in eighths, for a total of seven valley folds. Turn over.

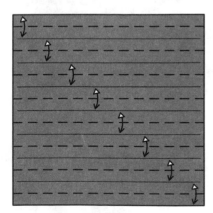

2. Divide the paper into sixteenths by putting a valley fold in between each mountain crease.

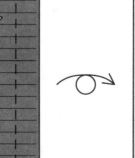

3. Now divide the paper into eighths vertically, making the valley folds perpendicular to the existing creases. Turn the paper over.

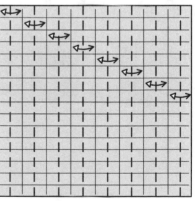

4. Put a valley fold in between each mountain crease from step 3.

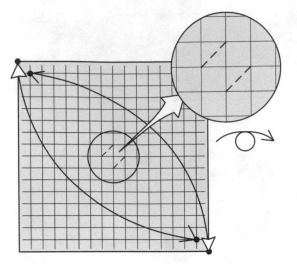

5. Following the arrows, pinch two tiny valley creases in the center. Then turn the paper over.

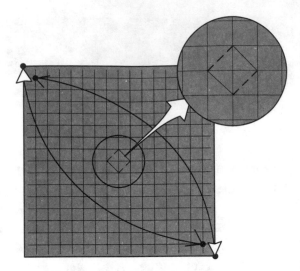

6. Following the arrows, pinch two more tiny valley creases in the center.

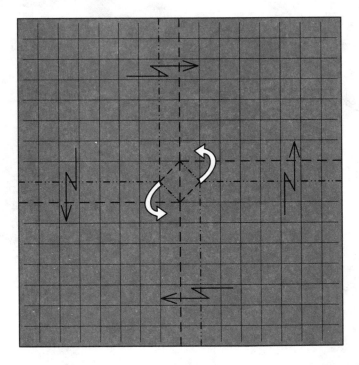

7. Using existing creases, make the indicated mountain and valley folds. This will cause the little square in the center to make a quarter turn. The paper will not lie flat.

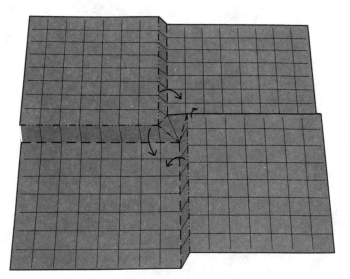

8. This shows the twist in progress.

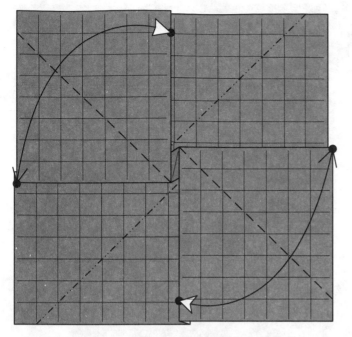

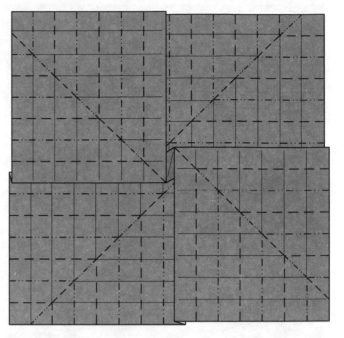

9. Following the arrows, make the diagonal valley creases. Repeat behind for the mountain folds. Note that these creases do not hit the corners of the model. Crease all four creases in both directions (mountain and valley) for easiest assembly.

10. Make the indicated folds starting from the center and moving outward. The diagonal folds will get formed naturally by squeezing together the existing horizontal and vertical folds. Twist the center, making the sides come together.

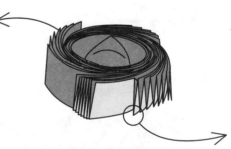

12. Finished Flasher. Pull the corners of the Flasher apart and together to make it coil and uncoil, providing a "flash" of the central color. If you make the Flasher from heavy, springy paper and store it coiled up (held by a rubber band, for example), when you stretch it out and let go, it will coil up on its own.

11. In progress. Wind up the center, curling the edges around the outside.

Spring Into Action

Designed by Jeff Beynon

This model is conceptually quite simple, but it is the hardest model in this book to assemble. However, the effort is well worth it at the end. Your paper must be very crisp and a bit heavier than normal bond paper. Take particular care with the precreasing — even one wrong crease can sabotage the model!

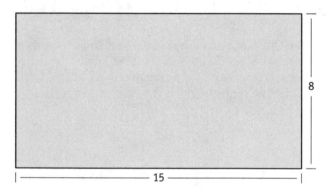

1. Most origami models start from squares, but this one begins from a rather unusual rectangle in the proportions of 15:8. The next few steps show two ways you can make a rectangle of this proportion.

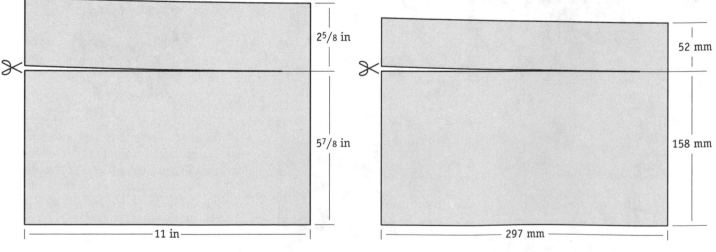

2. You can make this from a sheet of American letter paper (8$\frac{1}{2}$ by 11 in) by cutting a strip 2$\frac{5}{8}$ inch wide off of the long side.

3. You can make this from a sheet of A4 European letter paper (297 by 210 mm) by cutting a strip 52 mm wide off of the long side.

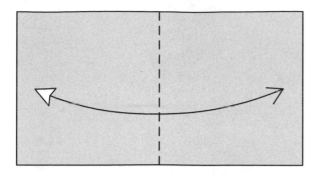

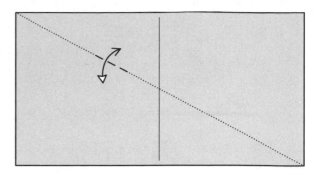

4. Make sure the white side is up. We're now going to divide the rectangle into thirds both ways. Steps 4–6 show how to find a reference point by folding, but if you still have your ruler out, you can just measure it if you like. Fold the paper in half from side to side and unfold.

5. Fold the paper along a crease that runs between the upper left corner and the lower right corner; you only need to make the crease sharp about 1/3 of the way along.

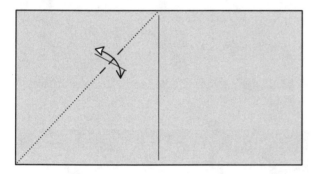

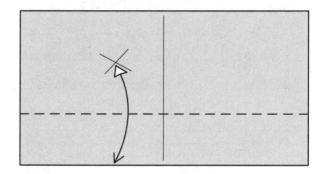

6. Fold the upper left corner down along a crease that runs from the lower left corner to the middle of the upper edge and unfold. You only need to make the crease sharp where it crosses the one you just made.

7. The intersection of the two creases is 1/3 of the way down from the top and 1/3 of the way from the left edge to the right. This method works for any rectangle. Fold the bottom edge up to touch the crease intersection and unfold.

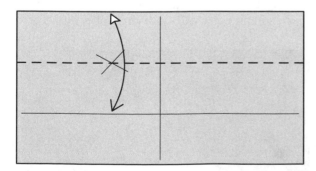

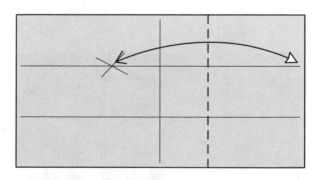

8. Fold the top edge down to touch the crease you just made and unfold. (The new crease should go right through the intersection of the two reference creases.)

9. Fold the right edge over to the crease intersection and unfold.

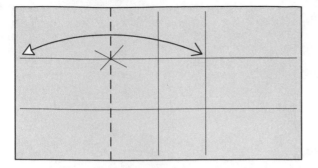

10. Fold the left edge over to the crease you just made and unfold.

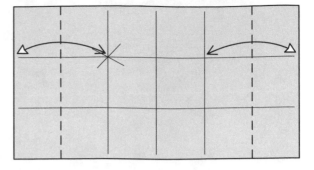

11. Fold the side edges in to touch the existing creases and unfold.

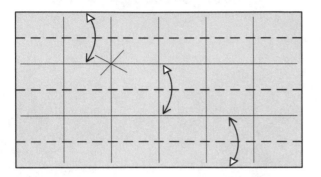

12. Divide each of the horizontal panels in half.

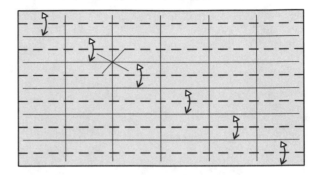

13. Divide each of the horizontal panels in half again.

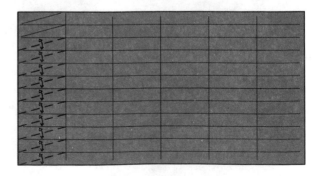

14. Turn the paper over.

15. Crease the upper left rectangle along the diagonal with the crease running from lower left to upper right. You can accomplish this neatly if you first lightly score each rectangle along its diagonal using a blunt point, such as a dry ball-point pen.

16. Repeat on the next panel down.

17. Repeat on the remaining ten panels in the column.

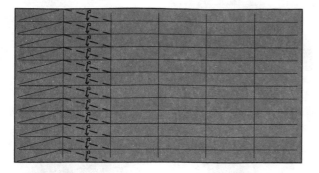

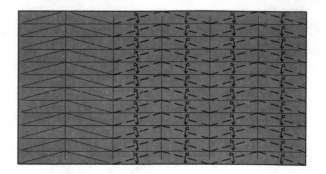

18. Repeat steps 15–17 on the next column, but with the crease on the other diagonal of each panel.

19. Repeat on the remaining 48 panels.

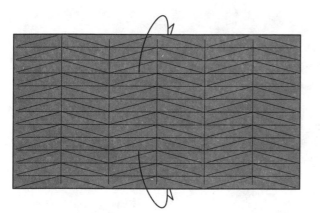

20. Curl the paper into a tube and turn it over.

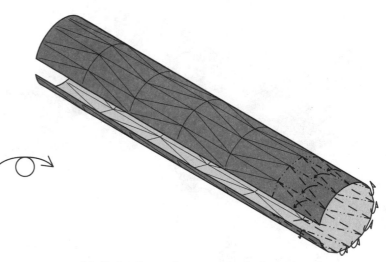

21. Twist the end counterclockwise using the existing creases. You my find it easier to use a cardboard tube as a support while you do the twists.

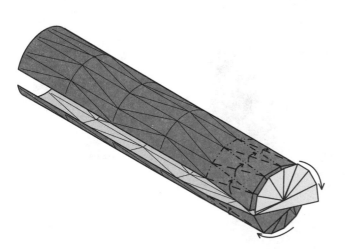

22. Now twist the end clockwise, again using the existing creases. You'll find it very difficult to get all the creases going at once, but when they're all started, it will pop into place.

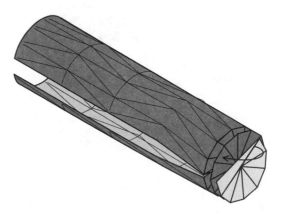

23. Without undoing the twists, bring the white layer out from inside the end.

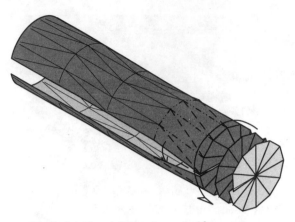

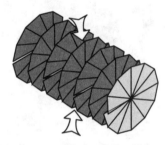

The middle disk slips inside itself here.

24. The twists should now form two separate disks on the end of the tube.

25. Twist the right end one-half turn counterclockwise using the existing creases; make sure you tuck the upper edge inside the pocket as you do.

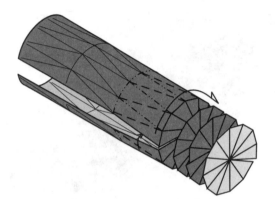

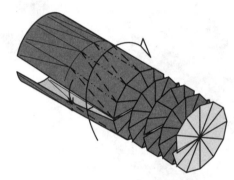

26. Twist the right end clockwise on the existing creases, this time making sure that the lower edge goes inside the upper edge.

27. Repeat steps 25–26 on the remaining two segments.

28. Squeeze the middle disk to activate Spring Into Action. See step 29 for a different view.

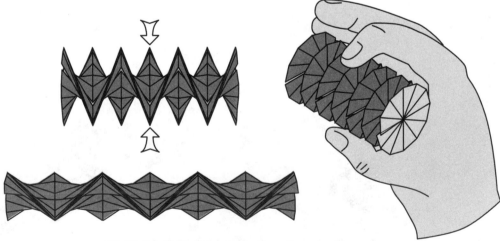

29. Finished Spring into Action. Squeeze the center of the model to make the sides spring out. The model works best if you use somewhat heavy paper and store it compressed (for example, under a heavy book) before springing it.

Acknowledgments

I would like to thank the many folders who contributed their wonderful designs, without which this book would be but a shadow of its present form. Several people brought to my attention particularly interesting action models, including Jan Polish of Origami USA and V'Ann Cornelius. Scott Griggs of C&I Photography spent many patient hours taking the photos for both the book and the cover. A special thank you goes to Sam Randlett and Gay Merrill Gross, who made a thorough and careful reading of the original manuscript, caught innumerable mistakes (including some excruciatingly embarrassing ones!) and made many helpful suggestions. Many more mistakes were caught by proofreaders and proof-folders of individual models, notably Tom Hull, Diane Lang and the expert staff at St. Martin's. Needless to say, any mistakes that remain are entirely my own. Particular thanks goes to my editor at St. Martin's, Joy Chang, who has indeed been a joy to work with and who shepherded this work through the entire production process with unflappable good cheer!

Sources

If you would like to learn more about origami, you might consider joining one of the international origami societies. There are many such groups worldwide that hold conventions, exhibitions, teach special sessions, and publish magazines, newsletters, and books containing the latest advances in the art, as well as the names and addresses of regional groups around the country and around the world. For further information, send a self-addressed stamped envelope with two first-class stamps to any of the following:

Origami USA
15 West 77th Street
New York, NY 10024-5192
U.S.A.

British Origami Society
c/o Penny Groom
2a The Chestnuts
Countesthorpe
Leicester LE8 5TL
England

Nippon Origami Association
1-096 Domir Gobancho
12 Gobancho, Chiyoda-ku
102 Tokyo
Japan